Dedication

This book is dedicated in part to the millions of black people, who lose their lives at the hands of hatred, because of many white people who held and still today, hold hatred in their hearts toward black men, women and children.

Dear Parents,

*How do you answer the question of race
when your kids ask it?*

Dear Teachers,

*How do you handle such a sensitive subject
in your classrooms?*

*I've written this book to ask the questions,
so you have a way to give them the answers.*

Keith M. Hammond

White Hatred Black Hope

Overcoming Oppression in America

Cover Layout and Interior Design: Keith Hammond

Lessons For Life Books

LESSONSFORLIFEBOOKS.COM

LessonsForLifeBooks.com

Unless otherwise indicated, any and all Scripture quotations are from the Holy Bible, King James version. All Rights Reserved.

A Lessons For Life Book

White Hatred
Black Hope

Overcoming
Oppression
in America

© 2016 by
Keith Hammond
is published by
Lessons for Life Books, Inc.
St. Paul, MN 55116

DISCLAIMER:
None of the pictures or images contained in this book belong to the author. Many thanks to the originators and owners for the use thereof.

No part of this book may be reproduced or utilized in any for or by any means, electronic or mechanical, including photocopying, recording, or by any information storage or retrieval system, without permission in writing from the Publisher.

Inquiries should be addressed to:
permissionrequest@LessonsForLifeBooks.com

ISBN-13: 978-1-938588990
Printed in the U.S.A.

Table of Contents

Section One - By Force

Chapter One 19
- Kidnap Them Away From Their Loved Ones 20
- Move Them to a Land Their Families Can't Reach 23
- Enslave Them and Kill Those Who Won't Comply 26
- Make the Slaves Work All Day for No Pay 29

Chapter Two 33
- Pass Laws to Make Slavery Legal 34
- Form Classes to Set the Status Stage 38
- Deny Them the Right to Vote 42
- Kill them and Refuse to Prosecute the Killers 46

Chapter Three 51
- Treat the Slaves Inhumanely Sunup to Sundown 52
- Kill Any Slaves Who Attempt to Escape Captivity 56
- Rape Women and Children to Make the Men Obey 60
- Create Organizations That Promote Oppression 64

Chapter Four 69
- Call Them Names So They Know You Hate Them 70
- Pass Laws to Prevent Access to Any Resources 74
- Make it Illegal for Them to Learn or Earn 78
- Create Organizations That Promote Oppression 82

Chapter Five 87
- Create Discriminatory Policies and Procedures 88
- Post Signs to Remind Them They're Not Welcome 92
- Charge Convict and Imprison Them on False Charges 96
- Ruin Their Reputation With False Reports 100

Chapter Six 105
- Refuse to Comply With the Proclamation 106
- Deny Them Loans for Housing and Businesses 110
- Steal Their Inventions Products and Plans 114
- Kill Them People When They Protest 118

Chapter Seven 123
- Control Lawyers and Judges To Get Convictions 124
- Prevent Earning a Living Upon Release From Jail 128
- Make It Legal For Landlords To Discriminate 132
- Make It Difficult For Employers To Hire 136

Chapter Eight 141
- Give Them Guns Drugs and Alcohol But No Jobs 142
- Have Media and Filmmakers Portray Them Negatively 146
- Keep Killing Entire Generations of Their Families 150
- Segregate Them in All Facets of Society 154

Chapter Nine 159
- Work Diligently to Crush Their Hopes and Dreams 160
- Secretly Use Them to Test Drugs and Viruses 164
- Monitor and Sabotage Their Every Movement 168
- Call Anyone Who Tries to Help Them 'N-Lovers' 172

Section Two - By Fear

Chapter Ten 179
    Use Torches and Molotov Cocktails to Destroy Their Homes 180
    Dress Up in Hoods and Lynch Them to Enhance Their Fear 184
    Burn Crosses on Their Lawns to Deny Their God and Their Faith 188
    Kill Their Leaders to Make Them Fear Speaking Out 192

Section Three - By Faith

Chapter Eleven 197
    Faith Hope and Charity 198
    Love Your Enemy 202
    I Will Lift Up Mine Eyes To The Hills 206
    Fret Not Thyself Because of Evildoers 210

Section Four - Epilogue

Chapter Twelve 217
    Summary 218
    Poem 220
    Resources 221
    Hope and Anecdotes 229
    Closing Thoughts 245

This work is Comprised of History, Hope and Anecdotes
and Suggested Solutions for a Better America.

All Rights Reserved.

VIDEO EXCERPT

In addition to the 245 pages of incredible insight in this ground-breaking book, here is the video of the author from 2014 that accompanies this work.

White Hatred Black Hope
VIDEO #30
LINK: PastorKeith.org/whitehatredblackhope

In this video Author Keith Hammond, gives insight into how white hatred has fueled black hope for centuries.

Here is an excerpt:
I'll start this lesson at the place where white Americans with hatred in their hearts want people to believe they began this lifelong quest to conquer, which is the 1400s.

But the reality is that in the 1400s whites from abroad came here claiming they discovered America, but the natives already lived here.

And rather than leaving the natives alone or helping them grow as a people, so the two cultures could find a way to live together in this vast land, white greed & selfishness caused them to destroy the natives with methods that included guns and alcohol.

Such destruction is how whites have worked diligently to destroy entire generations of black people with segregation, lynching, guns, drugs, alcohol, threats, and incarceration.

I could talk for days about the false claims of more discovery in the 1500s; or the exploitation of native land by forced colonization in the 1600s; or how when the natives refused to assimilate, whites decided to swindle those who fell for it, and kill those who didn't.

NOTE:
Starting on page 221 in this book, there are links to approximately 30 more videos on this subject from people whose viewpoints are worth noting.

POEMS

White Hatred Black Hope

Close your eyes if you can,
Imagine yourself as a black woman or man.

Kidnapped away from your native land,
With no explanation or way to understand.

Stolen and taken across the sea,
Your intentions were to instill servitude in me.

To enslave us and make us work for free,
Oppression and slavery are what they will always be.

Your way is to enslave and oppress,
Our method is prayer, patience, and kindness.

POEM

Coupled with the ability to love you in spite of your deep-seeded hate,
Martin said 'I have a dream' and that vision sealed his fate.

Through the canal of oppression emerged a people gifted and great,
To stand black and proud believing freedom can never come too late.

Yes, you lynch and shoot those who refuse to comply,
Killed their bodies but their souls didn't die.

They live on as martyrs in our consciousness and memory,
When the glory comes what they died for will finally set us free.

You still oppress us in the year two thousand sixteen,
Our fight for freedom and equality is now on every screen.

You're no longer able to hide under hoods and masks,
Being exposed is what will allow you to be taken to task.

One after another our people still die,
And everything you say is based on a lie.

Columbus didn't discover America in 1492,
Natives caught him trying to steal as you always do.

Show up and claim that this is now your land,
Like everything else you do, unsavory and with slight of hand.

Believing that no one will notice all that you do,
But now the joke is starting to be on you.

People of all colors are standing up for what is human and what is right,
So the fight to end oppression is no longer just black folk's fight.

POEM

What's done in the dark will always come to light,
Supremacy is now inferior, replaced by colors other than white.

So this is no longer a passionate plea,
Because you can no longer stand on top of me.

You can no longer keep me from being free.
I'm worth much more than being allowed in the house for tea.

My voice trembles with the cries of people before me,
Screaming for us to open our eyes so we can clearly see.

The one reason you still want to destroy me,
Is because I am what you can never be.

When you look at me you focus outside on the color black,
I look at you and pray you'll see what's inside me is what you lack.

White Hatred Black Hope

You filled our communities with guns, liquor stores, and dope,
We flocked to the churches to express our faith and embrace hope.

You can't destroy us because you never could,
Oppression is but a mirror that reflects your evil and our good.

White men killing black men...so what else is new?
The only difference is the cameras, exposure, and unity too.

You can kill our bodies and even lock us away in a hole,
But you can never kill our hopes, dreams, and certainly not our soul.

Torches and threats never really made us fear or fret,
It made us pray harder knowing that God was not done with us yet.

POEM

Never repay evil with evil, but instead respond with what is good,
That's really tough when my people were hung up on a piece of wood.

You exchanged nooses and ropes for a badge and a gun,
We evolved into a people who stand, fight, and no longer will we run.

Loving your enemy is right and biblical but it's never easy,
Because every time I think of my ancestors and my children I get queasy.

There's a fading list of things you can do to oppress me,
One day your hatred will be nothing more than a bad memory.

This poem was therapeutic in spite of all that you have done wrong,
It gave me strength, stamina, and endurance, and freedom won't be long.

Love is the spirit within which I write.
It is also what gives me the will to continue the fight.

INTRODUCTION

Where Do You Start?

To start the discussion of race I believe you have to abandon any and all of the past attempts to do so. I subscribe to the notion that in order for anyone, especially white Americans to have a dialogue about race or racism, or racial profiling, or being racist, or any of the categories in and around this sensitive subject, you must discuss it beginning with the truth and reality of where slavery began, which is in the early books of the Bible.

If God sanctioned slavery, He did not approve abuse of power. Once we're willing to discuss the facts around Egyptian rule of the first slaves, the exodus, the plagues and other fallout such as God wiping out the entire Egyptian army, behind a Pharaoh who abused his power, only then can we start to dialogue about the reason for modern-day slavery, and move the discussion on to the next stages, which is the native and black Americans.

In the entire scope around this issue, people, the media, and anyone who is focusing on this topic, tends to ignore where and how America began. Everyone of course, except the natives.

There were two cultures of people affected by slavery not just ONE.

And no amount of reparations via classifications as sovereign nations can remove the past even if you cover it with casino cash.

Before Africans were forcefully brought to America, natives lived here. Their native lands were invaded and stolen, all in the name of greed, and they became slaves to the bottles of alcohol they received in exchange for an entire country. In our minds, and in the media, we tend to ignore it, thinking their classification and casino payoff covers it, but the reality is that another entire culture of people will never fully climb out of the pit of enslavement they were put in long before Africans were.

If God approved slavery, He did not sign off on the abuse of such power. But somewhere, some way, somehow, European explorers ignored that fact, and took it upon themselves to use the very foundation of sanctioned slavery, tossed out its intent to teach people how to submit to God, to benefit man.

The exploration, forced colonization, dividing of the nation, and assimilation of native and African people into a society that abused one group for their land, the other for their labor, proves and shows us that although the Bible eludes to not despising humble beginnings, these beginnings were anything but founded out of humility.

They were birthed through canals of stealing, killing, and destroying, which the Bible says is the work of the Devil. We know that what the Devil means for bad, God certainly turns it around and works it out for our good. His infinite wisdom stepped in and used the situation to usher in mass education and inspiration through Christianity.

It took centuries for Native Americans to receive payment for their lands, but Africans, now Americans, have yet to see any pay for our labor. And in my humble opinion, it should be tenfold because of the pain and suffering we endured at the hands and whips and nooses and torches and chains and laws and lies and words and many other sorts of degradation and segregation.

Will we ever be free? Will we ever be equal? Will we ever be compensated?

Surviving all that African-Americans have gone through from the first people who were kidnapped from Africa and brought to this country, to today where we have witnessed the election of the nation's first black President, still begs to answer the questions: Will we ever be free? Will we ever be equal? Will we ever be compensated?

People may ask how these things can ever be, given the seemingly endless graphical representations of the remnants of the past we personally know has never been behind us, because we live with subtle and even glaring indications of it every day, shown through the continued killing of unarmed black men, black women, and black children.

How can these things ever be?

The plight of our people will forever continue on in the tears and memories of those who have lost loved ones and endured pain and suffering in this never-ending struggle.

Electing a black President surely is a step toward progress, but it is not nearly enough. We could take additional steps toward equality by breaking open the doors to institutional racism and systemic injustice and removing them from their historic hinges.

I still remember watching black and white television with my dad as a young boy, and seeing the national guard standing with weapons drawn while black people entered a building just to go to school. I still remember asking my dad, *"Will the police be there when I go to school too?"* and seeing the dazed look on his face as he drew on every ounce of strength to keep the tears in his eyes from rolling down his cheek. *"No son, we escaped the south to move north."*

Today, I think about how naive his answer to my question was in thinking that by moving north, he'd somehow escape the hatred that continued to spread like gangrene all over the country and still, 36 years after his death in 1980, has yet to be overcome.

We shall overcome has always been the battle cry of black folk. But we know that in order to do so, many white people will have to be moved, pushed, and possibly even forced to step aside. 'Clear and Present Danger' may have been a movie in theatres, but this title is the reality of black life daily.

In my flesh, I wish to time travel back to slavery so white Americans can witness the torture, and see firsthand how what they did to us still affects us. But in my spirit, loving our enemy and forgiveness moves all of us forward.

Thus, I remain hopeful that we will overcome, but as you read through the chapters of this book, know that these are simply mirrored reflections staring each of us in the face as we look for modern solutions to centuries old problems.

I remain hopeful that reparations will be done.
I remain hopeful that victory will be won.
I remain hopeful that one day, glory will come.

Section One

BY FORCE

BY FORCE

Oppression
White supremacy and the idea of superiority within the white race was the tool employed and the method engaged to use against other groups of people to keep them in a state of mind and matter as chattel, working for free, suffering as human beings, just to give others a false feeling of being elite.

Suppression
Keeping their foot firmly planted on the necks and heads of those they oppress is how they kept their hopes and dreams suppressed. They use internal networks and hidden agendas to work a master plan to help ensure that they will always be supreme and their race would remain pure.

Regression
Each and every time black people work together or form a collective or talk of a way to unite our people, many whites with hatred in their hearts find some way to try and take us backwards so that any effort made to move forward is simply branded as a one-hit wonder rather than true progress.

Aggression
Historically, whites kill what they cannot control. This is what we are seeing played out on camera phones today. The issues being exposed have always been there, but the cameras haven't. In the past, the lynching, the wars, the all out effort to destroy natives and black people was systematically hidden.

Obsession
God gave each group of people a separate continent to live on. Only when whites became greedy and were not satisfied with the status quo, did they set out on this quest to conquer that which belonged to everyone else. This obsession still exists today, but it has morphed into taking it by any means necessary, regardless of who it hurts in the process, all in the name of progress.

CHAPTER ONE

KIDNAP THEM AWAY FROM THEIR LOVED ONES

Africa is full of a diaspora of cultures, classes, and citizens, The natives of which were originally all black. Today, that society is being speckled with whites who by reason of being offspring of their parent's research, and other premises such as the same platform they used to invade America, rarely if ever has it been a white person 'wanting' to move to Africa and live in the bush.

On most of the continent, as it has always been, there is still no electricity, no running water, no toilets, no windows, no heat or air conditioning, no jobs, and so on. To think that any European or white American individual or family is going to just pull up stakes from the creature comforts of their homes and plant them in Africa seems a stretch, except the missionaries who started going there to do mission work and then return to the comfort of their homes.

It is noted in many history books, regardless of how inaccurate or blatantly dishonest it may be, that in the mid-millennium, the period through the 1400's and 1600's, explorers set out to 'discover' new nations, seemingly because they weren't satisfied with the land where they were living, or greed pushed them to a place where they felt they needed much more.

During their exploration they discovered that there was an entire continent of black people who walked around naked, lived in huts with no creature comforts, and lived among the wild animals. So the label they put on them was 'savages'. Instead of leaving them to their way of life and sailing on the next continent, in the name of 'exploration' they followed the wickedness in their hearts and what they believed were biblical instructions.

This started a path and set the course for Africans being captured, killed, and kidnapped away from their native land, their families, their way of life. Compassion was not the order of the day. White people had guns. Black folk had rocks and spears, but no knowledge of how to use them in a war against weapons of mass destruction, to defend their way of life and freedom.

The result was that white explorers wielding weightier weapons prevailed, and Africans were kidnapped from their loved ones and forced into slavery.

Kidnapping an entire culture of people away from their loved ones meant literally destroying the very fabric and foundation of that African nation. It meant forcing oneself into a society that seemed content in their condition.

Africa is a protected continent. Look at its history. There are no tornados. There are no hurricanes. There are no blizzards or snowstorms. There are none of the many devastating natural disasters that plague literally every other part of the planet. Africa is a protected land.

You may think it's because of where it sits in relation to other continents, but I believe that it is because life began there, humanity originated there.

Greed is the Gangrene
that makes people do some strange things.

Earth is a huge planet, and even with billions of people inhabiting it, we still have only to colonize a small portion of it.

Asia is still largely unsettled.
Africa is still largely unsettled.
Europe is still largely unsettled.
Antarctica is still largely unsettled.
Australia is still largely unsettled.
North and South America are still largely unsettled.

However, whites start wars against everyone else because greed still to this day pushes explorers to a place of being unsatisfied with their piece of the proverbial pie, and they would rather covet what their neighbors have, and set themselves on a course to conquer in order to feel like they're in control.

White people on the planet, are the plague of this planet. Not all of them, just the greedy ones. I'll say this until the day there is no more breath in my body. Their actions speak louder than any words I could ever utter. And until they repent and recompense for their actions I will never trust them.

Kidnapping people away from their loved ones is an unspeakable action. It is much worse than cruel and unusual punishment.

Kidnapped for being black.
It's illogical. It's intrusive. It's incomprehensible.

Throughout the centuries when people being kidnapped from Africa and brought to America the very culture of the African people changed. Whites who enslaved them introduced their own seed into the mix by raping the women and producing children of mixed race.

Centuries of this process birthed an entirely new culture, which are mixed black people in America and mixed black people in Africa today.

The result of such abusive and intrusive action led into and laid the very foundation for Genocide and Apartheid, which spread the emergence of the elite onto yet another group of people whose human and civil rights were already being violated, essentially duplicating the same atrocities that began taking place in America.

In African Apartheid, the government sanctioned segregation, separated education, and created yet another superior vs inferior mindset in the lives and across the continent natively owned by black people.

White people are greedy, global gangsters. And while many of them grow and learn to abandon their inherited ways, the idea of white privilege still permeates every facet of their existence whether they subscribe to it or not.

MOVE THEM TO A LAND THEIR FAMILIES CAN'T REACH

Kidnapping wasn't the only plan, the next step was to move them to an entirely new land. A land that was thousands of miles away across the sea, where no African could ever get to or ever reach.

Many men and women were taken from their native land, forced into ships that carried them across waters that only served to separate them from the family they knew and the life they were accustomed to.

Travesty doesn't begin to describe the tribulation, and even though the process of assimilation began centuries ago, we're still witnessing the negative and irreversible effects of it today.

Many people including presidents have tried to put an end to or make amends for the historic hell that African and now black people have been forced into, but the efforts will never be enough to cause global change.

Who had the very first thought to kidnap people and move them away from their families and native land?

Who do you think had the very first thought to kidnap Africans?

What do you think prompted them to think that way?

When do you think it happened?

Where do you think they were when it happened?

Why do you think they chose Africans instead of any other people?

How do you think the African people who were left behind in their native land where their loved ones had been kidnapped felt, dealt with, and carried on with their lives? Words cannot do justice to or adequately explain their pain. However, we can start to examine the process from the beginning and see where it leads us.

The African continent is where Egyptians are, and where the Bible says Moses was. But prior to a deliverer being used to emancipate people from Egyptian rule and slavery, nearly everything in the Bible points to the Garden of Eden being somewhere in Africa.

If you believe Biblical history, the Africans, namely Egyptians, were the ones with the power, the authority, and the warriors. Africa is still the only place on the planet, where most of the original animal species roam freely, other than zoos which have developed over time.

To look at this issue from the beginning of slavery, we have to draw from the research and resources available to answer the questions. Let's take a look at the map to help respond to the following:

<u>**Who**</u> <u>do you think had the very first thought to kidnap Africans?</u>
While the who isn't documented we do know the how. Looking at the map, we see that for hundreds of years, Africans were the commodity within the slave trade. Africans were used as free workers to pick cotton to be marketed and sold as a product throughout the world that would only benefit whites.

<u>**What**</u> <u>do you think prompted them to think that way?</u>
Greed is typically the basis for any type of action that causes one person or a group of people to mistreat others in order to monetize themselves.

<u>**When**</u> <u>do you think it happened?</u>
We don't have to guess this one, because ship logs and maps have been uncovered to give the timelines that those who participated can't.

<u>**Where**</u> <u>do you think they were when it happened?</u>
Studies show and I believe they originated in Europe, mostly England.

<u>**Why**</u> <u>do you think they chose Africans instead of any other people?</u>
Africans were unable to fight back or defend themselves against guns and other weapons. They were taken into slavery to be sent to pick raw cotton, and other items, which were then shipped back to Europe to be manufactured and processed, then it was sold as goods all over the globe. Slaves were also forced to work in other capacities, all to benefit white folk.

Overcoming Oppression in America

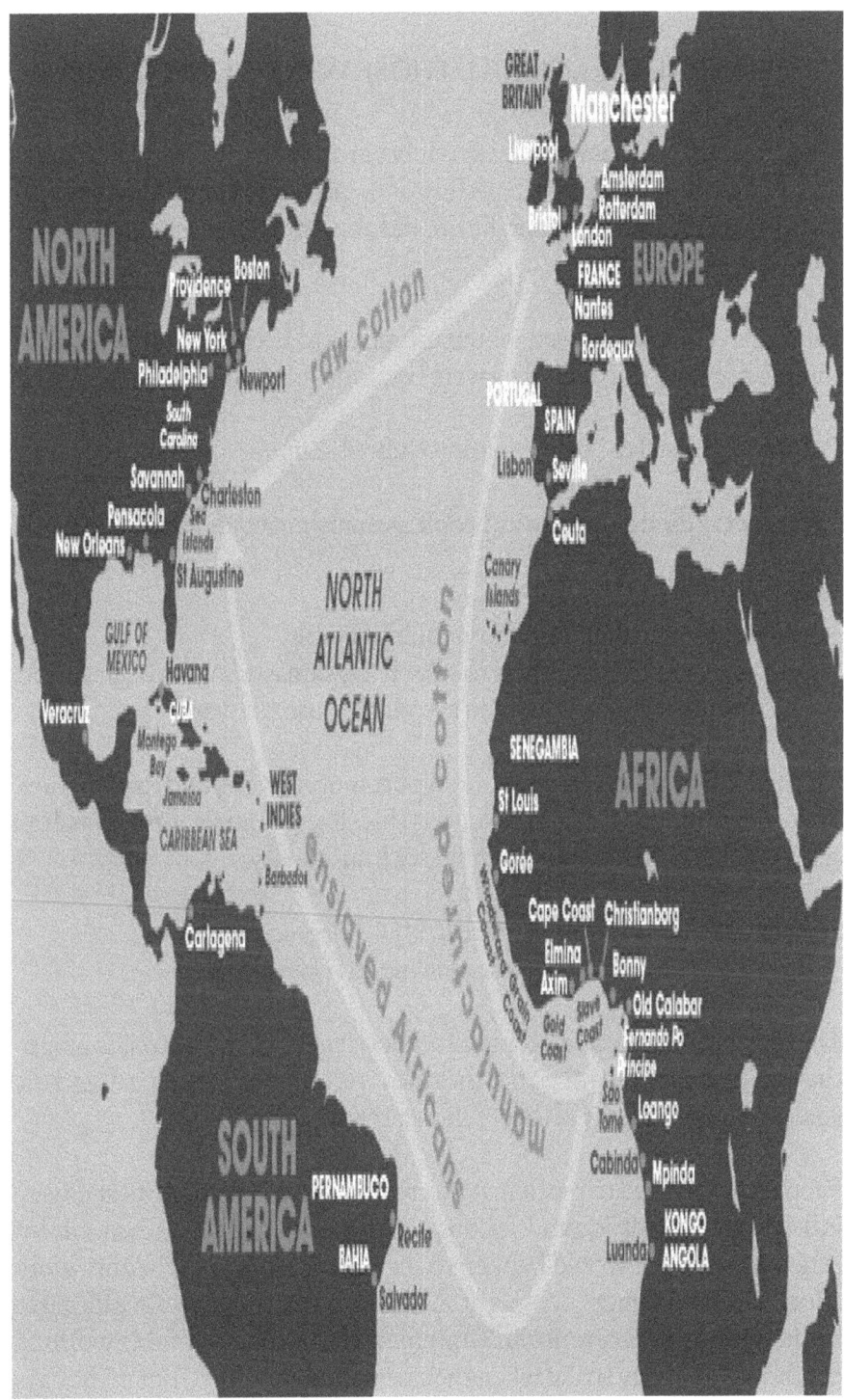

ENSLAVE THEM AND KILL THOSE WHO WON'T COMPLY

Slavery is not a new concept. It began in the early days of humanity but those who participated in it as the slave owners, took it to another level, as greedy humans generally do, and abused the power and authority they were given.

Taskmasters typically used inhumane means to keep slaves in line and in compliance with the work they were being forced to do.

Whips were used to beat people into submission.

Chains were used to lock away people as punishment for refusing to work.

Murder was used for many reasons:
+ To put fear in workers who wouldn't comply.
+ To set examples for others to see what taskmasters were willing to do.
+ To punish those who couldn't work or refused to work.

Killing millions of black people for sport is cruelty beyond explanation. There is no compassion in acts such as this. There is no remorse in such an action. There is no reasoning behind such an activity.

Compliance is the act of following the rules conforming to the established set of standards.

The problem with forcing people into following the rules and conforming to the established protocol is that the rules were and still are illegal, and the standards only benefitted those who set them.

People who refused to participate were considered antagonists and were killed for their attitude and actions or tossed in jail to set an example for others to see what would happen to them if they joined in the anti-work effort. The punishment doesn't fit the crime when the laws were illegal to begin with. Workers unite and unionize against unacceptable working conditions and they strike when their demands aren't met, but in the days of slavery, this wasn't even an option. The status quo was for blacks to either comply or die.

What seems quite strange to me is that the slavemasters must have thought they had an endless supply of blacks to force into slavery because in all the research I've done and all the stories I've heard, murdering slaves for breaking the rules was commonplace.

While murder was often used as a last resort, after merciless beatings did not force someone to comply, each and every individual whose life was taken meant that the taskmasters were losing an item from their inventory; and subsequently suffering the financial loss attached to the value of that person.

Murder that was never acknowledged. Murderers never held accountable. Entire generations of family members simply done away with. Buried in unmarked graves. Even the records that may have been able to identify and provide some closure to those left behind, destroyed.

> *The Bible is very adamant about history and genealogy.*
> *The U.S. Census is quite clear on counting and logging data.*

Time capsules, in whatever form they come in are essential to ensure that those who come after you are given the information about their progenitors.

I remember watching the trailer for the movie *Amistad* for the very first time. I was moved by the images of men in chains being beaten into helping to rowing and righting the ship. The scenes invoked a sense of compassion for the enslaved, but also provoked long buried anger at the atrocious actions.

My dad taught me to bury my anger, lock it away and throw away the key. He sensed my disapproval of the images on television news and special reports showing glimpses of the reality of how black people were treated.

My anger, while deeply buried in a chasm behind other feelings of grief from all the death that took place in our family over a period of time, simply served as the kindling needed to spark the fire within to compel me to want to do something to not only help right the ship, but dream of taking it over.

HOPE AND ANECDOTES

- **Admit** that what was done to slaves was wrong.
- **Accept** responsibility for the actions and the resulting fallout.
- **Apologize** to the descendents of those who were killed.
- **Atone** for the sins by monetizing the slaves sacrifice.
- **Agree** to make laws to make it impossible to happen again.
- **Abolish** any laws that still exist that were illegal to begin with.
- **Arrange** for sensitivity training for everyone who benefitted.

---

*What can be done to reverse the reality
that slaves were killed when they refused to comply?*

Many of those who initiated and participated in the slave trade may be dead and gone. Those who subsequently benefitted from these abhorrent actions pretty much includes every non-Jewish white person on the planet.

But how do you hold them responsible, and can you? They only reaped the rewards of their forefathers, they weren't the chains that caused the problem.

Is there anything that can be done to provide retribution to those who are descendents of slaves who suffered? Is there anyone who can be held responsible for the recurring nightmare that haunts those who still hurt behind their family members being killed.

*How do you prosecute murder that was never acknowledged?
How do you bring to justice murderers that were never held accountable?
How do you provide closure for entire generations of family members?
How do you locate those buried in unmarked graves?*

The improbabilities are infinite and only add more salt to wounds that are impossible to heal, but you cannot work on a wound until you are first wiling to remove the bandage.

MAKE THE SLAVES WORK ALL DAY FOR NO PAY

Jobs are for people who have been hired to do them. The task may be anything from sweeping floors to cleaning toilets to cooking meals to picking cotton. Whatever the work, everyone who does it deserves to be compensated for it. *Every worker is worthy of their wages.* Biblical concept but the construct is as simple as it sounds.

In the days of slavery payment was refused to slaves who worked tirelessly in jobs such as picking cotton or being servants to their slavemasters. Those who labored all day were forced to work for no pay.

In their native land of Africa, even today, workers in villages where jobs do not exist generally share in the spoils they are able to collect or gather. If they are out in the bush trying to catch dinner for the day, when they are successful, everyone within their circle within that village is able to be fed.

On most other continents, back in the days of slavery, workers typically received at least room and board and a meal when there were no wages of any kind to offer the workers.

The practice of forcing people to work for no pay has not ended unfortunately in the prison systems in America. Having been to jail more than once I've personally experienced firsthand working all day for the substandard wage of $.25 per hour.

To the contrary, I've also been employed by the very prison system wherein I was incarcerated. I was hired as a Technology Specialist II and worked at the women's prison in Shakopee, Minnesota. My salary was in the mid thirties so it was quite ironic when I ended up on the other side of the law.

I've also designed and built a high school where I had 30 staff people that I paid substantial wages to, and I recently owned and operated a bookstore where I paid employees as well. I've earned anywhere from $50 to $150 an hour working under technology and consulting contracts over the years, but to be forced to work all day for no pay seems completely foreign to me.

Although it seems in 2016 that such a practice should have been abolished long ago, unfortunately there are parts of the world where workers are forced to work for no pay or even substandard wages.

Whether it is in sweat shops or textile mills, or in labor camps, or inside a federally funded and sanctioned prison system, this practice of forcing workers to slave all day for no pay should be banned.

I find it interesting that America, as a nation, now has policies and laws against such practices but actually actively supports them within the prison system and labor camps.

I'm reminded of some of the current news reports I see glimpses of where a group of laborers fighting and protesting for higher wages and for a vote to be placed on the ballot so people can make the decision rather than let the same non-livable wage practice and policies continue to plague society under the power of white authority.

People are fed up with being forced to work jobs where they cannot make a living off of what they earn. As a capitalist society, America needs to level the playing field in that workers should be worthy of their wages, and those wages should be raised to a level where it can benefit the workers instead of keeping them living below the poverty line.

I've learned over the years that I've been studying this issue that people who are at the top typically do not care about those at the bottom. Once they've made their mark financially, everyone is basically on their own. This attitude of *I've made mine now you make yours but until you do, I'll pay you pennies* is dangerous in that it continues to feed into the notion that people with lots of money, regardless of how they got it, are somehow better than those who don't have any. This elitist attitude is much more destructive than effective.

This notion is how American started down the path of slavery to begin with. It's an ideal whose time has come to be overthrown. Upended in a sense that leveling the playing field would benefit the masses, rather than just having a small group of individuals with all the wealth, all the power, and all the ability to make decisions that affect the rest of society.

HOPE AND ANECDOTES

+ **Change** laws and policies to elevate workers above the poverty line.
+ **Correct** the mindset that capitalism is better than inclusion.
+ **Conform** to a wage model of that benefits workers and their families.
+ **Challenge** every person in power to participate in equal pay practices.
+ **Comply** with the living wage labor laws once they are enacted.
+ **Compensate** workers with a livable wage so it benefits everyone.
+ **Cooperate** with agendas and efforts to level the playing field.

---

*What can be done to reverse the reality
that slaves were forced to work all day for no pay?*

American society was built on the backs of slaves who were never compensated for their labor. Many of their descendents and blacks throughout history and even in our current society were forced to suffer in, under, and through the resulting fallout.

Today's society is based on the commodities and value within the gross domestic product system. Given that slaves were once treated as a product traded within this system, where those who owned the produce made the money and the slaves received none, it is my unwavering belief that the descendents of those uncompensated slaves, which means basically every black person on the planet, including American and African, should be given due compensation for the free labor that whites profited from on the backs of black people.

This is the only way in my opinion to level the playing field. However, just giving black people millions of dollars today will not solve the problem. White people must adopt the practice and abide by the laws and policies that it is unfair to force someone to work for no pay, little pay, or wages that keep them below the poverty line. Until this happens, no amount of reparations will ever be enough.

CHAPTER RECAP

+ Did the previous chapter teach you something?
+ Were you moved to want to want to help in some way?
+ Do you see any possible solutions to this issue?
+ Did these facts give you better understanding?
+ Does the hope suggested below offer apt solutions?
+ Share Comments: @WhiteHatredBlackHope

HATRED
Kidnap Them Away From Their Loved Ones

HOPE
Their loved ones are likely gone, any descendants would have to be found, though sites such as Ancestry have begun to make an impact.

HATRED
Move Them to a Land Their Families Can't Reach

HOPE
Returning black people to Africa would completely complicate things, but we believe spending eternity in Heaven will enable us to heal.

HATRED
Enslave Them and Kill Those Who Won't Comply

HOPE
The United States government needs to step up and do more to officially put an end to slavery and not only make it illegal to kill people because of race, but enforce laws when it happens especially with closet racist cops.

HATRED
Make the Slaves Work All Day For No Pay

HOPE
Reparations would be a monumental gesture, but an official apology and signs of unity, solidarity, inclusion and integration would be a milestone.

CHAPTER TWO

PASS LAWS TO MAKE SLAVERY LEGAL

Laws that supported and promoted slavery were enacted and placed on the books and even enforced by various facets of government. These unjust laws served as the standard for American society for centuries.

The fact that the laws were based on illicit motives and actions made the laws suspect and borderline if not outright illegal to begin with. Anyone who held to these sadistic standards and are still making an all out effort to hold on to them is not to be trusted.

White Americans have been privileged for centuries regardless of whether or not they subscribed to the notion. Laws were created to promote and protect the prescribed purity and prominence of the white race.

Passing laws to make and keep slavery legal was the foundation that made for abuse and atrocities that continue to this day. Quite possibly, the entire U.S. Government was complicit in these actions in the days of slavery, and it is my belief that many of them are still diligently working to take things back to the way they once were.

Slavery was illegal regardless of who says it was. It is not humane to own another human being. It is not moral to sell another human being. It is not at all legal to oppress an entire culture of human beings based on the color of their skin. And, I don't care who says it such laws are illegal on their face.

As a member of this society and a natural born citizen of this country, I have the right to voice my opinion about such matters. I have the ability to do so especially when I'm compelled into standing up for what is right because of the actions of others.

Slavery was wrong back then and it still is today. Anyone who participated in it then should be jailed and possibly hanged, since that was their favorite form of eliminating black people back then. Eye for an eye, tooth for tooth. Fortunately, repaying such evil with more evil simply feeds into the evil. Instead, we must forgive, respond with good, and continue to strive for much better social constructs and societal interactions with other humans, and white people should be the first ones to sign up for this class.

When researching this book and the various topics contained herein, some chapters were more difficult than others to deal with. There were many times I had to step away from my keyboard when what I was typing resurfaced so many of the conversations I had with my dad about these issues.

It served as a reminder of us watching Alex Haley's Roots together and him asking me questions about why I was crying and why my fists were clenched during certain scenes.

Many of my responses, as honest as they were, simply opened the door for him to look deeper into my heart and to examine my character on a much broader spectrum.

> *How many people in our family were killed and tortured?*
> *Why would anyone do this to another human being?*
> *Why didn't our people just fight back?*
> *Why are these people so evil?*

The answers to these age old questions were very poignant back then, but still ring true today.

> How many people in our family were killed and tortured?
> *There's no way to know how many were killed and tortured.*

> Why would anyone do this to another human being?
> *We've been asking ourselves the same question for centuries.*

> Why didn't our people just fight back?
> *It was a losing battle to fight against their weapons.*

> Why are these people so evil?
> *We've always believed that the Devil has a lot to do with it.*

No matter how right my dad's answers were, they still leave more questions.

According to several statistics such as those contained in the Trans-Atlantic Slave Trade Database, 12.5 million Africans were shipped to the New World. 10.7 million survived the dreaded Middle Passage, disembarking in North America, the Caribbean and South America.

These statistics are staggering just to think about but it gets even more egregious when you consider the additional 4 million that may have died inside Africa who fought being captured, or once they were captured, before they reached the port for passage.

At the point where we begin to discuss this issue in town hall meetings, or in the senate hearings where they should be, we must first request and or require the leader of this *free* world to stand before the people and acknowledge that these acts were horrific.

Horrible is not even close to describing how it makes me feel each and every page I type and every dream I have or movie trailer I force myself to sit through.

My wife and kids can tell you that it has taken me decades to just sit and watch movies or TV shows that depict black life during slavery. It is still too difficult for me to deal with the facts behind it.

However, as a responsible parent I needed to show my children the world we live in, and the reality of what they would be facing once they were old enough to get married, have kids of their own, and eventually have to make the decision to share the same information with their own children.

My daughters are both grown and married now. They have blessed us with four grand-kids, and they both work in professional careers. They work hard, obey the laws of the land, focus on their faith and family, and are doing what we taught them to do to keep from becoming a statistic in this seemingly never ending fallout from slavery.

What I taught them I pray they will teach their own because the lies their kids will be told and taught through the very books contained in the schools they attend, need to be corrected when they get home, as I did with them.

HOPE AND ANECDOTES

+ **Allocate** funding to develop support groups to deal with black PTSD.
+ **Apply** faith and forgiveness philosophies to help people heal from hate.
+ **Associate** hate crimes with war crimes and prosecute them as such.
+ **Alter** our actions in this area by providing more support systems.
+ **Adjust** our thinking about slavery by abolishing all remaining laws.
+ **Adjudicate** the perpetrators of hate crimes without bias.
+ **Amend** the pattern of letting secret grand juries oversee hate crimes.

What can be done to reverse the reality that laws were passed to make slavery legal?

It is my humble belief that every child starting in every junior high classroom in this country needs to be taught American history from the perspective of the truth rather than the lies and rhetoric that is contained in many of the history books today.

As someone who designed, built, and opened a high school in 2000, I'm keenly aware of the disparities in the history books yet they still remain a part of the basic standards required to graduate.

Rewriting history books to include the truth, regardless of how damaging, is a necessary component to moving forward and making progress in this country, unless of course we don't care about the truth, and would rather slavery remain a dark and unacknowledged part of our past, rather than a proponent of the growth and development of our children's future.

Until and unless we own up to our past, any future we hope to achieve will remain bleak and biased. America was once a very prejudiced nation, and glaringly, many parts of it still are. Fortunately, white America is becoming the minority and people of all colors are moving to the front of the line as the majority.

FORM CLASSES TO SET THE STATUS STAGE

Class in its very form was never a part of early North America. Natives believed in hierarchy based on the chieftain system and structure rather than a class-based one.

The following classes became a guideline for American life during slavery and are still prevalent in today's society:

NO CLASS
Un-classed people in America unfortunately are still labeled this way. They are mostly undocumented workers and immigrants, illegal or otherwise. This classification was developed to help keep *these sorts* of people in their place, which is why there has never been any real effort to develop a modern, modified, manageable method for illegal immigrants to become citizens.

LOWER CLASS
People who have always been considered substandard were and still are the Negroes of our society. Black people were branded this way and are still thought of and treated this way by many White Americans regardless of how much money we have. Those who live in ghettoes and just happen to be black are considered part of this sector of society. I'll leave trailer parks out.

MIDDLE CLASS
If you have achieved what many call the American dream, which includes and is not limited to college graduation, quasi-suburban home ownership, 2.5 kids, and careers to help you support it all, you are officially, albeit a fictitious moniker, part of the middle class. Add in a pet, good schools, and membership on the board of a social or grass roots organization and voila.

UPPER CLASS
Turning the class-based system on its head are those who drop out of high school, create companies that become monopolies in their industries, and make more money than ever thought possible. This of course is par for the course in the upper echelon of society, or the 1% of 1%. Just below them are those who can afford to keep up their image in this status-based set.

WORKING CLASS

For argument's sake, let's say this is the vast majority of Americans. They are blue-collar, hard working people who care nothing about fitting into or being conformed into any one of the classes. They are the farmers and auto workers, transit personnel and countless other labor-driven titles that do not follow or fit into the status quo perse.

Inheritance has enabled many white Americans to maintain their status in this class-based society. Regardless of how the wealth was obtained, given that the vast majority of white American wealth was gained on the backs of blacks, or by paying low or no wages to other groups of people, or via another means such as theft from various corporate coffers or ponzi scheme, rarely was the wealth of the past based on invention or hard work.

In my opinion, once you allow someone to inherit what was stolen from others, it should make those who receive it in the future just as culpable as whoever left it behind. It truly boggles my mind that the wife of Madoff was allowed to keep millions stolen from investors; this truly boggles my mind.

A class-based society does not mean that it is the way things are, it is simply the way that those in power *think* you and others are. Those who created this system always will consider themselves at the top and worthy of being there, regardless of what elevated or carried them there.

Given that history shows most used the steal, kill and destroy method to reach the pinnacle, in my opinion they should be on the bottom of the ladder in a new category deemed *subclass*.

Every person who ever arrived in the United States pre-slavery and during the stealing of land from Native Americans can be considered to be here illegally. Thus the argument against illegal immigrants is an asinine one.

Since natives are technically the only true citizens of this country, none of us can make the argument that anyone else is not welcome here. We are all from other countries. We may have been born here post-invasion, but unless you are Native American you are not a naturalized citizen of America, you are simply a colonized one.

Colonies and classes have been the basis of many factions, cliques, sects, and even wars in this society. Such groups exist in nearly every facet of American society and no segment seems to be immune.

For example if you're a member of a country club, most of which were at one time white only, any many still are, you're considered upper class. However, if you're a member of the Boys and Girls Club you're considered lower class.

Such dynamics have no place in any society but America has established this course and set this standard in order to consider itself far above and ahead of the pack, when in reality it isn't. We are far behind many others in many areas such as education, integration, and social support. Even our neighbors to the north in Canada are far more advanced in many areas including and not limited to health care and gun control.

We don't have to live in a class-based system, but we rarely leave what we are born into. Many Americans have defected from the status quo and have chosen to live their lives off the grid so to speak. This is simply because they understand that status has absolutely nothing to do with what is in your heart and the way you are supposed to treat other human beings.

It is far more important to fear God and eschew evil in this life, and working hard to maintain ones status is simply a symbol of those in power to keep those who want status willing to step on anyone and do anything to get it.

There are television shows that prove this theory in that they exist solely to follow a family around and show their daily activity as if they are what is right with our society when in fact it is quite the opposite.

People who flock to watch, follow, and like those who have their lives scripted for the public to access, have been hoodwinked into wanting their lifestyle and are willing to do anything to get it, including tossing their morals out the window.

This class-based culture is responsible for so many systems being in place from slavery all the way to bullying because those who are enslaved or bullied may not fit into what others deem unworthy of their self-indulgent class.

HOPE AND ANECDOTES

+ **Remove** any stigma in place portrayed by the media about classes.
+ **Remind** your children often that keeping up with the Joneses is a farce.
+ **Release** information about the damage this class-based culture causes.
+ **Repair** any damage by teaching your kids to be content and modest.
+ **Recover** from a class-based system by getting rid of most items.
+ **Relocate** from class-based housing to much more modest means.
+ **Refer** to everyone you know for who they are and not what they have.

---

*What can be done to reverse the reality
of the damage this class-based culture has caused?*

Much of the damage this class-based culture has caused unfortunately still continues to this day. Reality shows have become the norm in the lives of those who would have an anxiety attack if they could not get a daily fix.

Hollywood has become a haven for how to discriminate against people based on class. It has produced addicts who are obsessed super-fans of the tweets, sound bites, and instant pictures, people who are gullible to the glitter.

I was taught from an early age that *all that glitters ain't gold*. I learned over the years after my mom and dad passed away that the love of money is the root of all evil. I taught my children not to covet what others have but rather pray for God's will to be done in their lives so He would bless them with what He wants them to have, and when they get it to be content with it and don't ever use it as a means of putting others down who have less that they do.

America's class-based culture is wrought with ways to be led around by the proverbial ring in many noses tied to a dangling carrot that offers nothing more than disappointment because the people they are being led by are not leading them to a better future, but rather simply using them to keep their egos fed, and on the top of the mirage that is the status ladder.

DENY THEM THE RIGHT TO VOTE

Voting is a fundamental right of all citizens. At least is should be. But this right has not always been in place. In fact, until the Voting Rights Act was enacted into law in 1965, black people never had the right to vote in America.

This means that from 1789, when the very first President was elected until 1920, one hundred thirty one years, the only people who were allowed to vote in elections were white men.

In 1920, women received the right to vote. It took an additional forty five years until 1965 when black people were granted the right to vote. Unfortunately, we are still fighting the battle of voting fraud and ballot corruption even half century later in 2016.

> *Power tends to corrupt, and absolute power corrupts absolutely.*
> *Great men are almost always bad men.*
> *~John Dalberg-Acton~*

Denying blacks the right to vote kept us out of the power structure.

Denying women the right to vote kept them submitting to their men.

Voting helps level the playing field in many ways:
+ To help keep democracy at the forefront of politics.
+ To put fear in politicians who know they can be held accountable.
+ To engage the people in elections to promote democracy.
+ To provide a platform for people to use their voice.

Denying people the right to vote has kept white men in power far too long in America. I've always wanted to run for office, but as a felon I'm prohibited from doing so. White men who held the reigns to my release know this so they placed insurmountable obstacles in my path in the form of decades of probation on top of the time I served to keep me from ever entering politics so I could become part of the solution to this white men only problem.

As a black man, I know my vote doesn't count even if I could cast it. Even my dad knew this. The people don't elect the President, a small group of officials who are controlled by the wealthy and powerful, elect the President.

This is a rigged system that has been in place far too long. The results of this hidden hierarchy are starting to surface and showed itself in the 2000 Presidential election when the candidate who received the popular vote was not elected to the Presidency.

While I am not now nor have I ever been a fan of politics or politicians, I do understand the need to make changes from *within* the system. Force tends to instigate a fall, which typically is the reason for pockets of people protesting but historically it has not been enough to effect long-term change.

White men in America have been in political power far too long. This is changing, but it has been a long slow process. The change that is taking place is birthing new candidates, from different cultures, with new ideals, and a passion for helping people instead of padding their pockets. I believe the reason white men still fight diligently to keep control of the political process is because so many Bills are approved into law without the public ever voting on them or even hearing they exist.

This is how politicians have made themselves and their cronies rich for centuries. Their ability to sneak Bills through underneath or inside other Bills has been their way of doing business far too long and until and unless it is abolished and new, honest, people are elected into those political offices, it will continue to be *business as usual with party politics*.

American politics is and always has been a corrupt and rigged system to help keep white men in power. Again, as a black man, I know firsthand the ways white men have developed master plans to keep black men out of power and the political process by making certain that as many of us as possible have felonies attached to us. This has been part of the overall plan and process that takes away black people's right to vote for decades. White men have a history of being the plague of this society, and until and unless this structure changes, the battle for equality, voting rights, human and civil rights will rage on with little results.

Another reason I believe the political system in American needs to be overhauled is because people need to know how dark and dangerous the process of lobbying is when it is used to control the way politicians vote on certain Bills.

Lobbyists know that the way to prevent Bills from ever being subject to a line item vote within the various committees is to lobby for or against the Bill at the bank. Throwing money at politicians has always been a way to buy their vote. Another level in this rigged system we call American politics.

For example, cigarettes most likely would never have become a product sold to Americans had it not been lobbied for approval at the political level. The manufacturers knew the product caused cancer, and I believe the politicians who they had in their pockets were informed as well. Money and wealth and power has always taken precedent over the lives and well-being of people in this country.

Another example are the drugs that manufacturers have been allowed to push into pharmacies via the political process. The manufacturers know the drugs are addictive but the power of their lobbying keeps politicians in their pockets, which helps ensure approval.

America needs help in a very bad way. My hope is that God Himself steps in and puts a stop to the endless levels and layers and lies of corruption at the top, that exist within and around our own government. I mentioned earlier that the love of money is the root of all evil, and unfortunately, America has been a truly evil nation far too long.

This doesn't mean it can't change, but it will take an *act of God* to make it happen. Politicians don't fear the people, they work for us, but they have no fear of being un-elected. Too much power exists once they are in office and the temptation and long-standing business as usual structure grabs hold of them and often never lets go.

I have been discussing my interest in political office for many years with people who are inside, but my passion for being a pastor and leading people to a life in Christ, outweighs any passing interest in politics.

HOPE AND ANECDOTES

+ **Regulate** laws when they are enacted to benefit black voter's rights.
+ **Reform** the current rigged political systems to include the people.
+ **Remove** centuries old policies and protocols that exclude voters.
+ **Reprimand** anyone including officials still using corrupt systems.
+ **Rework** the political systems at the state and federal levels.
+ **Redevelop** best practices as a standard that ensures voter inclusion.
+ **Report** abuses that occur after new systems are in place.

What can be done to reverse the reality of being denied the right to vote has caused?

Ask almost anyone these days and they will tell you that the political system in America needs to be overhauled from the top down. Unfortunately, the only way to do this is to remove and rework the rigged system called the Electoral College, and the monetary juggernaut called Lobbying.

Both of these political processes are responsible for the deaths of millions of people in America and until and unless we are angered behind these facts we won't work to abolish them.

There are people inside who are diligently working to change the system from within. And they are genuinely good people who believe things can be better and understand how to help make it happen. But the system they are fighting has been entrenched and entrusted so long that it is nearly impossible to make lasting changes.

Sure, change happens on the surface, but enforcing those changes can often take years to make any real impact. And by the time it kicks in, white folks in power know that most people will have forgotten about the issue and moved on to the next fight therefore, business as usual continues on as the standard set by this corrupt political process hundreds of years ago.

KILL THEM AND REFUSE TO PROSECUTE THE KILLERS

Protests have been taking place for decades in this country to bring attention to violations of civil and human rights. People in general are showing that they are fed up with the old ways of abusing power and people are raising their voice by taking to the street and social media.

When you are in a position of power as a public servant you abuse the public's trust when you kill someone and are never prosecuted for the crime. I didn't say take someone's life in self-defense, I said kill someone. There's a distinct difference.

The problem in this country is that the practice of killing black people for sport has been taking place far too long. White men have killed more black people since the days of slavery than they could ever atone for. In fact, as I mentioned in a previous chapter, a national database places the numbers around 12 million.

These are all murders without prosecution. If they tried to do that in someone else's country, it would be an all out war and people would be sacrificing their life and limb to try and stop it. That's the action and attitude that needs to take place in today's society. People need to stand up and fight for what is right.

Police officers are not all bad. The ones who join the force simply to use it as a protective covering around the hatred in their heart have been rewarded for doing so and that is wrong. When police cross the line and commit murder they should be prosecuted to the fullest extent of the law. And, it is my opinion that they should be immediately placed on Death Row so they can never take the life of another person.

Crooked police officers do not fear the people. They do not fear God. They don't fear prosecution. This is a very dangerous cocktail waiting to be lit and tossed onto the pathway of innocent people. This process of protecting the police even when they are clearly in the wrong has to stop and when the prosecutors don't do their jobs, they need to be fired just the same.

Refusing to prosecute such offenses is the biggest slap in the face to black people both past and present. Every once in a while we'll see a token white man tossed to the public for prosecution and we'll let our guard down slightly and start to believe things are changing for the better.

This is a false reality that is designed to give us false hope. Prosecutors are not inclined to hold police accountable for their actions. We see patterns of it littered across the country and no community is immune. When even body cameras and cell phone video does not serve as sufficient evidence in such crimes we know that we are in serious trouble.

Personally, I have never feared the police. I hold the utmost honor and respect for them because of the jobs they do, but let me be absolutely clear, my feelings are for those who actually serve and protect, not those who wear a badge and carry a gun to cover up the hatred and racism in their hearts.

How do you vet racist applicants from the police academy entry process? It is nearly impossible given that they hide it oh so well. In the past, they used hoods to cover their faces because they were too coward to let it be known that they were the ones who burned a cross on your lawn or threw a Molotov cocktail into your window.

Today, they don't have to hide. They have a license to kill with government and departmental support to back them up when they do. This is a travesty of justice that puts honest and honorable police in the middle of a long-standing battle where they shouldn't be. They are forced to make a decision to stand up for a fellow officer, or another white man, against the crime they commit. Difficult decision but a necessary one. Unfortunately, those who make these decisions get it wrong more often than not.

I simply pray for the souls of everyone involved because I believe there will be a day of reckoning, a day of atonement, a day to stand before God and give an account for everything they do. And not standing up for what is right when another officer commits a crime makes everyone just as culpable as the guilty officer themselves. Prosecution of crooked police is a start but it has to carry over to the prosecutors who refuse to do their jobs as well. And we cannot stop there, we must include members of secret grand juries also.

Police brutality has escalated into murder. Both rarely get prosecuted and both of the positions involved, namely the police officer who commits the crime, and the prosecutors who protect them from prosecution need to be in jail, with no possibility of ever digging up the key.

Anyone who knows me understands that I have three retired Chicago police officers in my family. Thus, my respect level for the jobs they do exceeds that of any normal adoration.

Anyone who knows me also understands that I practice forgiveness first. As a man of God, I value everyone's life as if it is my own. If someone confesses and repents, they are forgiven indeed, but that does not preclude them form prosecution for their crime. Sin is one thing crime is another. Sometimes the two intertwine, other times they do not.

The law of God is one thing, and the laws man create are another. God is going to hold us accountable for each and every law of His that we break; but man has a tendency to ignore both God's law and man's law, which is why even if you are forgiven by God and by man for a crime you commit as a public servant, you must still face the music and be prosecuted to the fullest extent of the law.

For the first time that I've ever paid attention, we now see black men begin taking it upon themselves to retaliate against police officers who unjustly kill black people. This has always been an all out war, but Dr. King proved through the non-violent actions of the civil rights movement that violence is never the answer. We cannot and should not repay evil with evil.

Some people believe that the only way to send a message to police officers is to take some of their lives. This is wrong. There is never any excuse to become *like* the people you are trying to send a message to. If you kill after they kill, you are no better than they are and you should be prosecuted right along side of those officers who break the law.

Citizenship in America and the 2nd Amendment may give you the right to bear arms, but that does not mean you need to exercise it. I'm all for protecting ones family, but not if I need to brandish a weapon to do so.

HOPE AND ANECDOTES

+ **Install** citizen review boards to vet anyone who applies to be an officer.
+ **Improve** relationships with residents by including them in the process.
+ **Instill** public confidence in police officers using various measures.
+ **Incorporate** prosecution as top priority when police commit crimes.
+ **Inject** federal review boards to prosecute and process at county levels.
+ **Infuse** communities with satellite police stations that welcome citizens.
+ **Inspect** prosecuting protocols for loopholes and biases and close them.

What can be done to reverse the reality
of refusing to prosecute murderous police officers continues to cause?

I've often wondered about people who protest after an acquittal or when yet another black person gets murdered; why they set fire to their own communities instead of finding out where the people who committed the action lives, and taking your anger out on them rather than yourself.

It seems completely asinine to me that anyone would destroy and loot and take away the resources in their own communities, when the perpetrators of the crime that upset you likely live outside your community, in the suburbs. They sit at home and watch your anger play out on their televisions.

I'm not a proponent of violence but it makes more sense to me that if you're going to react, take it out on the individual(s) who committed the offenses rather than the innocent merchants and residents of your own community.

Refusing to prosecute crooked police officers makes the prosecutors just as culpable. It all needs to stop. Racist white men have been getting away with such crimes far too long, and the only way to make it stop is not with murderous retaliation, but by raising your voice, using your vote, and making certain that change takes place from within the system so that the corrupt system doesn't continue to exist even when you remove a few bad apples.

CHAPTER RECAP

+ Did the previous chapter teach you something?
+ Were you moved to want to want to help in some way?
+ Do you see any possible solutions to this issue?
+ Did these facts give you better understanding?
+ Does the hope suggested below offer apt solutions?
+ Share Comments: @WhiteHatredBlackHope

HATRED
Pass Laws to Make Slavery Legal

HOPE
Abolishing these hate filled laws is the first step to healing from our past hurt. Until this is done, nothing else will matter much.

HATRED
Form Classes to Set the Status Stage

HOPE
The section on colonies and classes provides insight that most people are not aware of, even if they're caught in the midst of it.

HATRED
Deny Them the Right to Vote

HOPE
The United States government needs to step up and take responsibility for overhauling the antiquated political system. This system was created only to benefit white men. It needs to be thrown out and rebuilt for the people.

HATRED
Kill Them and Refuse to Prosecute the Killers

HOPE
The families of people who lose their loves ones to violence by police officers need closure. Fire the prosecutors and the officers and pay the families.

CHAPTER THREE

TREAT THE SLAVES INHUMANELY SUNUP TO SUNDOWN

How do you treat black people when you go to work? If you are black how do you expect to be treated when you get to work? Do you abuse your power when you are in supervisory positions over black people?

Do you make black people under your supervision do things that demean them?

Do you use office tools such as staplers to beat black people just to get them to work faster or harder?

Do you engage other white co-workers and expect them to mistreat black people the same way you do at work?

Do you pay black people less money or no money for the same jobs that white people are getting paid to do?

Do you give black people less benefits or bonuses for the same jobs that their white co-workers are doing?

Do you refuse to give black people bathroom breaks or lunch time at work?

Do you give black people much harder or nearly impossible jobs to complete at work just because they are black?

Do you make negative or degrading comments toward or about black people at work?

Do you put much more or undue pressure on black people at work who are doing the same jobs at their white co-workers?

Do you refuse to include black people in company outings and events?

Do you think you are prejudiced against the black people you work with?

Years ago my wife and I went on vacation twice to Memphis, Tennessee. The first time we went there with a national church convention so we did not get a chance to visit the one place I wanted to take her to see.

The second time we returned to visit some of her family that lives there. During the second trip I made my way to highway 61 and drove toward Tunica, Mississippi. Tunica is known as the slave capital of the U.S.

While the town has changed tremendously since the days of slavery, I wanted to show her the place where much of the cotton was picked by black people in the south. We were fortunate enough to see some of the fields, and also drove by many of the plantation homes still in existence there.

The silence in the car during our visit let me know two things: (1) That it evoked a certain thought process, which eluded back to slavery. (2) Even though the last cotton field had stopped operating over 40 years before that time, the thickness of the torture could still be felt in the air.

Slaves were treated with reckless abandon during the days of slavery. They were whipped, beaten, chained, spit on, yelled at, raped, and even killed.

The slavemasters took it upon themselves to degrade and demean slaves to get them to submit, to behave, to work. They weren't given bathroom breaks or lunch times. This wasn't a comfortable work environment it was pure hell. It was unimaginable.

My reason for taking my wife there was to visit her family but I also wanted her to see where they had lived for generations, and why, even though her grandma lived in Chicago with their family at that time, that place was the reason that each and every time she saw a white person outside her window she would visibly shake into near convulsion.

Trying to help anyone try and understand what the slaves went through in those days may be difficult, but in my opinion it is necessary in order to get even a little understanding of the hatred in the hearts of many white people. Today, the treatment hasn't really stopped, it's just much more subtle, hidden, systemic, institutional and political.

HOPE AND ANECDOTES

+ **Teach** people the truth about slavery instead of hiding it..
+ **Travel** to places where cotton fields existed and plantation home are.
+ **Touch** on difficult subjects to give people a glimpse of what slaves felt.
+ **Talk** about solutions to modern day maltreatment and make it stop.
+ **Take** preventive measures to ensure every unlawful action is exposed.
+ **Train** people to understand how to be sensitive to the plight of blacks.
+ **Transition** from a mindset of privilege and persecution, to acceptance.

---

*What can be done to reverse the reality
that slaves endured horrific working conditions at the hands of their taskmasters?*

Violence has and continues to serve as the catalyst for the creation of many grass roots organizations. For example, violence against women launched many domestic abuse shelters and prevention programs; violence against children birthed many child protection programs; veterans have VAs, etc.

But have you ever wondered why there are no slavery recovery programs or post traumatic slavery centers? Think about this for a moment. One of the most egregious sins against black people in the history of this country has never been enough to warrant or ignite people to fund such programs to support the fallout behind slavery even though maltreatment is still ongoing.

The lynchings and killings and inhumane treatment of black people went un-discussed and unprosecuted for so long that creating support systems or even support groups for the fallout behind slavery seemingly never entered the mind of most people. Possibly people just wanted to forgive and forget.

One could make the argument that this is the reason so many black people have flocked to churches as their place of refuge behind this American atrocity, but I beg to differ in that while church is a hospital for the spiritually sick, the trauma caused by slavery needs some other type of triage center.

The trauma caused by slavery needs its own triage center.

KILL ANY SLAVES WHO ATTEMPT TO ESCAPE CAPTIVITY

Harriet Tubman is credited as being one of the most effective people to help slaves escape from captivity to freedom via the Underground Railroad. The pathway was a place for slaves to seek passage and refuge during their escape attempts.

The harsh reality is that many slaves never made it. If they were captured they were often killed, and if they weren't they were beaten to the point where they probably wished they were.

No one should ever have to suffer under such conditions but the reality is that they did. Killing slaves who attempted to escape captivity was a regular occurrence. Lynching was typically the most common form of punishment and it was used as a way to send a message to other slaves so they wouldn't try the same thing.

Torture is torture. Murder is murder. Slavery is slavery. Inhumane treatment is inhumane treatment. There are no palatable ways to describe it. It is what it was and still is.

Imagine arriving to work one day
and the co-worker you are accustomed to seeing there
is not working but rather hanging from the ceiling with a noose around their neck.

Would that affect you?

Would it make you want to escape captivity
or continue to suffer under the inhumane treatment
so the same thing doesn't happen to you?

I cannot imagine what any slave must have thought, how they must have felt, how they endured what they endured on a daily basis, or even how they could possibly hope or dream that a better day would come. Many of the slaves never saw that better day. They were killed trying to escape captivity. And the people who committed the murders will never be brought to justice.

One of my favorite songs for healing contains these lyrics:

> *Surrounded by your glory what will my heart feel*
> *Will I dance for you Jesus, or in awe of you be still?*
> *Will I stand in your presence or to my knees will I fall?*
> *Will I sing Hallelujah or I will be able to speak at all?*
> *I can only imagine.*

The song brings tears to my eyes each and every time I hear it or sing it because I hold out hope that when I get to Heaven, if I'm fortunate enough to make it there, that I will see the scars and feel the forgiveness of the people who lost their lives in slavery.

I truly want to hear from their own mouths how they did it. What helped them to endure years of inhuman treatment before their death? How were they able to hold on to hope that things would change? What can they tell people who are still alive fighting this same battle in modern times 2016?

Indeed one can only imagine what it would be like to hear from those who were hurt, or even killed. How great would it be today to sit and talk with slaves who are still alive in 2016 who can tell us firsthand what they endured, how they suffered, what it means to be free today? Do they consider themselves free?

While our imagination can run wild on this topic I'm brought back to earth by the fact that my mind tends to wander to those who will never have to pay or atone for their crimes, at least here on Earth.

I can only imagine that they will have to stand before their maker and tell what they were thinking. Why they chose to take the life of another person? What was it that made them start hating black people enough to want to enslave and kill those who tried to escape?

Was it a matter of keeping up with the Joneses? Was it something that pushed them to their actions? Were they taught to hate from an early age? Did they have any compassion for black men, black women, or even black children? Did they even care how the people they were mistreating felt?

HOPE AND ANECDOTES

- **Host** town hall meetings to discuss the fallout of slavery.
- **Help** people to get beyond their PTSD from the incidents and images.
- **Heal** through support groups and open, honest dialogue.
- **Have** discussions about how lynchings and gun violence are both murder.
- **Honor** those fallen through annual programs and dedications.
- **History** will repeat itself if we do not abolish the laws from the past.
- **Hope** that God will comfort all those are affected by this atrocity.

What can be done to reverse the reality
that slaves were lynched for many reasons including trying to escape captivity?

Pictures of lynchings of black people hurt me. Do they hurt you?

Pictures of dogs turned on black people upset me. Do they upset you?

Pictures of black people being sprayed with water hoses anger me. You?

Pictures of black children crying unnerve me. Do they unnerve you?

Pictures of black slaves picking cotton disturb me. Do they disturb you?

Pictures of black slave families staring into a camera bother me. You?

Pictures of black people running to catch subway trains get to me. You?

Pictures of pregnant black women picking cotton touch me. You?

Dad, why are those men hanging on that tree?

He was running to catch a train my son, but they never made it.

Overcoming Oppression in America

Pictures of lynchings of black people hurt me. Do they hurt you?

RAPE WOMEN AND CHILDREN TO MAKE THE MEN OBEY

Violence against women and children are crimes against all humanity. In a recent interview of feminist activist Gloria Steinem by reporter Charlie Rose, she said one of the most profound things I've ever heard. Her statement was simple but so on point that it should be spoken across every sector of society still trying to heal from violence.

> *"These are Supremacy Crimes"*
> *- Gloria Steinem -*

What is a Supremacy Crime? The definition is simple, it is a crime by anyone who thinks they are superior over another person or group of people.

Most people have classified and categorized such actions as Hate Crimes, but in fact Ms. Steinem is right, they are Supremacy Crimes.

In the days of slavery in America and in Africa, white men who claimed to hate black people often raped black women and children as a way to get the men to obey. Such actions were satanic and sadistic and often included sodomy against young boys and adult men.

Supremacy Crimes are about power and control. What I have yet to get or understand is that white men already had all the power and were already in control, so why use rape of women and children as another form of torture?

It has long since been discovered that rape is not at all about sexual gratification, it is about power and control over the person you are committing this horrific act against.

Women and children are the most vulnerable in our society, which is why it does not serve to reason why someone in power and already in control would attack them with such aggression and anger.

I truly wish there was some way to go back to the days when this violence took place so the white men could all be held accountable for their crimes.

I was molested in 1972, the night my mom died. Violence against women and children still exists today. We hear about it and see reports of it in the news media almost daily. Most recently, in a cold case that was finally solved after 27 years, a young boy who was kidnapped from his loving family was found. The white man who took him, raped him, murdered him, and buried him, finally confessed and led authorities to the victim's remains.

These types of tragedies are all too common and the perpetrators in the vast majority of these matters are historically white men.

Take it up a notch to another type of supremacy crime and you find even more white men who are already in power and already in control taking their anger and aggression out on yet more innocent people in the form of mass killings in schools and theatres and other venues all across the country.

Supremacy crimes such as these were never heard of or documented until they began in slavery. The evil that emerged from their actions have spread like a disease into other facets of society and still continue to be prevalent.

Men, women, girls, boys, no one is immune from the violence and the life-long traumatic effects behind it.

The fallout behind supremacy crimes in slavery is still showing itself in lingering poverty, post traumatic stress, anti-authority, disobedience and disrespect of all kinds within the homes of many black families all over the world.

Racist white men may never know and most likely will never understand and rarely acknowledge the damage they have caused to an entire culture of people.

The irreversible effects of slavery and the violence against women and children may never be forgotten in the minds of those who suffered through it and the descendents who still live with the fallout in their homes.

I cannot imagine what would make any person have it in their heart to want to commit such acts against another person, especially women and children.

HOPE AND ANECDOTES

- **Dedicate** efforts to help prosecute hate crimes and supremacy crimes.
- **Destroy** barriers that keep people segregated and separated.
- **Deal** with the reality of black people's past with patience and honesty.
- **Develop** programs that provide support and are sustainable.
- **Don't** ignore and push aside the needs of black people still suffering.
- **Double** and triple the amount of opportunities offered to black people.
- **Doors** are meant to be opened, open them and don't shut blacks out.

What can be done to reverse the reality that women and children were raped while slaves?

On August 26th 1972 the night my mom passed away, they carried her away from our home in an ambulance with almost the entire neighborhood watching. I was nine years old.

That night I was molested by someone I trusted and loved. It was a relative. Most hate crimes and supremacy crimes are committed by people who have a need to have power over you or be in control of what you do.

I've always asked myself, what could I have done wrong to make someone who I thought cared for me, do that to me? I was a young, defenseless boy. What could I possibly have done to deserve it? I've never received any answers to my questions so I simply learned to live with it.

Many slave women and children never got the chance to live with it. They were killed and died in their conditions. They never had the opportunity to see their dreams of a better life come true. They never saw their hopes to one day be free realized.

People really do not know how dangerous racist white men in America are. Many pass it off as if it will get better but history shows us that it never has.

Overcoming Oppression in America

Why does this image threatens or enrage white men?

DENY THEIR HUMAN AND CIVIL RIGHTS

Things didn't get better, time just moved on. Life didn't get better for slaves, time simply never stopped to let them catch up to it. Many slaves died before the Emancipation Proclamation. After the Thirteenth Amendment was ratified by Congress in 1865, slaves were free by law, but that did not stop the fight for their rights.

> *"We must accept finite disappointment
> but never lose infinite hope."*
> *~ Martin Luther King Jr. ~*

In fact, it would take another one hundred years of continued inhumane treatment and the denial of human and civil rights before a concerted and collective effort would rise up. Many people, black and white and even some from other races and cultures joined in the effort of the Civil Rights Movement of the 1960's.

During this century long battle that came to a head in the fight for civil rights, *whites only* signs were affixed to everything from bathrooms to bars. The signs extended to water fountains and were prominent in most every merchant's window.

While the Emancipation Proclamation made black people free by law, most white people were not having it. They refused to cooperate. Compliance was not in the cards. Slavery and the selling and ownership of black people was a commodity that would affect their bottom line, and force many to seek new means of making money.

Unwritten rules were enforced even though they were against the law such as making black people sit on the back of the bus. Black people were not considered human and called savages so expecting white people to accept that black people are indeed people, was nearly impossible.

Denying someone's human and civil rights on the basis of the idea that white skin should automatically certify ones whiteness as superior is asinine.

I remember back to 1983, I was in Thomasville and Friendship North Carolina working on a project. It was about 5pm in the afternoon on a normal sunny summer day. As I was walking back from the area I had just finished working in, I encountered a middle-aged white male.

Seeing that he was walking toward me, I did what I was taught to do by my dad, I spoke kindly by saying *Good Afternoon Sir*. His response cut me to my core because it was the first direct, face-to-face exposure to racism that I'd ever experienced. His reply to my kind introduction was *I don't know what you're doing out here but Sambo you'd better be inside by the time darkness sets in*. It shook me to my core.

My dad had warned me about such things, but I had only been exposed to them on the television news reports sitting comfortably in his room during evenings when he and I would sit and enjoy time together. The fact that he had passed three years before this incident; the fact that I was hundreds of miles away from home; the fact that I had no protection around me at all.

Having grown up on the south side of Chicago in the Englewood community where gangs, guns, drugs, and jail were all a part of life in my neighborhood, I had no fear of this white man, but I knew in order to keep from being lied on, cheated, talked about, mistreated, or worse, hung on a tree with a noose around my neck simply because I was the right color in the wrong place, I simply looked him in his cold bloodshot eyes, turned, and walked away. I didn't even dignify his ignorance with a response.

A few hours later, two blocks from where the incident took place, outside the hotel where those of us sent there to work on the project were staying, the street lights were out. I stood outside to try and enjoy the night air. In an instant I saw a red pickup truck with its lights on coming toward me from around the side of the building. The front seat and the back of the truck was filled with white men carrying fire lit torches, and they were wearing white hoods on their heads. I was right in their path but where I was standing must have been in the shadows because they never even saw me. As the truck drove past me, I couldn't move even though I was doing my best to. I was frozen because I had just seen the reality of what my dad and I watched in those news reports.

HOPE AND ANECDOTES

- **Uproot** anything growing that is trying to rewind us to segregation.
- **Unite** via social media & other platforms to stay connected to the cause.
- **Unify** with other like-minded people in peaceful protest over racism.
- **Urgency** needs to be underlined due to the current political climate.
- **Utilize** every resource available to ensure that the fight continues on.
- **Un-educate** the mis-educated and teach them real history in America.
- **Use** prayer, patience, and persistence because it will eventually pay off.

---

*What can be done to reverse the reality
that black people continue to be denied human and civil rights in America?*

Be kind

Play nice

Don't hurt people

Stand up to bullies

Show respect

I remember all of these things that my parents told me almost every time I was going outside to play or headed off to school. I was just a young boy back then and anything outside the radius of my neighborhood seemed a continent away. What I didn't realize is that the civil and human rights of black people were being violated just a few blocks away.

In retrospect, it is most humbling to know that I'm still alive. I survived the lynchings of the sixties, mass incarceration of many around me in the seventies, crack epidemic that targeted my neighborhood in the eighties, and all that has plagued black people through the nineties, turn of the century, all the way to 2016. I haven't learned yet why I'm still alive when so many others lost their lives and are still doing so today, but I'll continue to pray, and do my best to tell the story so those who come after me can read it.

Overcoming Oppression in America

Some see protestors, I see more blacks for white men to mass murder.

White Hatred Black Hope

CHAPTER RECAP

+ Did the previous chapter teach you something?
+ Were you moved to want to want to help in some way?
+ Do you see any possible solutions to this issue?
+ Did these facts give you better understanding?
+ Does the hope suggested below offer apt solutions?
+ Share Comments: @WhiteHatredBlackHope

HATRED
Treat Slaves Inhumanely Sunup to Sundown

HOPE
In order to stop the inhumane treatment of black people in America those who are responsible for the treatment need to be removed from power.

HATRED
Kill Any Slaves Who Attempt to Escape Captivity

HOPE
The Underground Railroad provided pathways for safety and freedom. We must never forget the sacrifices our ancestors made for our lives to be better.

HATRED
Rape the Women and Children to Make the Men Comply

HOPE
Instead of physically raping women and children like they did in the past, today they are raping the women by killing their kids. If we don't stop the officers who are racist things are going to get worse before they get better.

HATRED
Deny their Civil and Human Rights

HOPE
Because this issue has been going on so long without much change, the only hope is that those in power will be removed once and for all.

CHAPTER FOUR

CALL THEM NAMES SO THEY KNOW YOU HATE THEM

Sticks and stones can break my bones but names can never hurt me. Whoever came up with this is uninformed and needs to rethink it. Black people in America have been called and are associated with so many names other than our own, that we need to look at a few of them to try and grasp why it still happens.

+ Nigger and Negro

+ Colored

+ Sambo

+ Boy and Jiggaboo

+ Monkey

+ Lazy

+ Baby Factory

+ Ape

+ Ghetto

> NOTE:
> Every American owes it to themselves to watch the video titled:
> **Who Is Black in America**
> Originally aired on CNN in 2013.
>
> Soledad O'Brien interviews several people of color about their roots, and the names they have been called. It's an amazing video.
>
> The link and reference is on page 223 of this book. Look for Video #12.

This is just a very short list of some of the most derogatory and widely used terms to denigrate, dehumanize, and degrade black people. Some of the words refer to the dark color and pigment of our skin, the pronouncement of some of our facial features, the deplorable conditions in which some of the generations of our families have continued to live post slavery, the number of kids we have and the frequency in which we have them; the lack of initiative some of our people seem to have in spite of being forced into these conditions for so long that generations of our people have been forever effected. It is our plight, it was forced upon us, and no one should be expecting all of us to climb out of it all at once or even over the next several decades or centuries.

Hatred made this bed and it has no other choice but to lie in it. The results of slavery will last for as long as we were enslaved. Just because the law made us free does not mean that all of a sudden the playing field was leveled and we instantly became products of the American dream.

It is insane and asinine thinking if anyone believes that once you've been:

called names for generations,
beaten mercilessly for generations,
lynched, hanged and killed for generations,
kept from learning and earning for generations,
forced into subservient conditions for generations,
locked away in jail under false charges for generations,
kept from obtaining loans or owning homes for generations,

that all of a sudden one generation after 1968 when the civil rights movement came full force against these atrocities, things should be OK and the playing field is leveled and there is no more racism or hatred or name calling or any sort of discrimination. We do not live in an open sesame society.

I'll say it again, it is insane and asinine to think that things have gotten any better for some of our people who are still in poverty, can't pay their bills, feed their kids, educate themselves, pull themselves up out of systemic injustice and stand up against the racist based laws and policies and attitudes and actions that still exist in this country.

It's 2016 and racist white men are still killing black people all over the country and being protected by their badges, guns, and cronies in office.

At some point we are going to have to face the reality that is has only been one generation since the march in Selma, and let us not forget that racist white men killed Dr. King because he was willing to stand up and speak out against what has been a long history of inhumane treatment in this country. I pray and plead daily for God to take me out of here and I've been waiting for decades for it to happen so I no longer have to see, hear about, or listen to the racist rhetoric spoken by the myriad of racist white people in this place we blindly call land of the free.

HOPE AND ANECDOTES

- **Prayer** changes things when we are all on one accord and of one voice.
- **Pause** for moments of silent prayer to remember the past and the present.
- **Patience** has enabled us to come this far, let us not stop moving forward.
- **Persistence** is what pushed us from the back of the bus to driving it.
- **Passion** only works when it is directed at exactly what needs to change.
- **Purpose** helps us understand our place in the grand scheme of things.
- **Power** can only be received when those who have it share it or lose it.

What can be done to reverse the reality that black people are still being called derogatory names in today's America?

In 2016 America, if I could possibly speak for all black people I believe the vast majority of them would say they are tired and fed up with the conditions we still live in and the direct, indirect, systemic and institutional racism that still exists.

It is really a shame that we're still going through this after centuries of being oppressed. What is it that white people in power believe will happen if blacks were in power? Do they believe we will turn around and treat them like they've treated us for the past 500 years?

Do they honestly believe that we would start calling them the names opposite of what they've been calling us for generations?

Do they honestly believe that we would pass laws to do to them what they've continued to do to us?

If I can speak for all black people most of them would say that they don't ever want **anyone** to suffer under the bigotry we have been forced to endure, not even those who are responsible for making it happen and those who are still paying dues to help keep it happening.

Overcoming Oppression in America

When you want to talk to me, come out from behind the mask.

PASS LAWS TO PREVENT ACCESS TO ANY RESOURCES

From the beginning of America white men had an agenda. They set out to colonize the land once it was in their possession and develop housing, shops, and provide people with other goods and services in and throughout the townships and villages.

When they formed the government to set the standards for how the people should be governed, black people were not included as part of the plan nor were we privy to the discussion. They had stolen the land from Native Americans, so the next thing they needed to do was build on it. They cut down trees to use wood to build buildings, so have you ever wondered why they so desperately needed cotton as a commodity, and why they needed someone other than themselves to harvest it?

Interestingly enough, there are many explanations floating around the Internet, but in order to not let the cotton be the focus, I'll move on and begin to discuss the human commodity instead of the textile one.

White America back in those days established themselves as a mirror image of what they left behind in Europe. Everything from dress to dialect mimicked the way they dressed and talked in Europe. The only difference is that there were no cotton fields in Europe to be picked.

When slaves became the workers used to cultivate cotton so that it could be sold to other places and nations abroad, profit became king. Since white men were already making huge profits from selling slaves, greed set in when cotton became a commodity.

Since they didn't have to pay the slaves any wages, they had no need to set standards for how slaves would spend their money. They only had to make sure that if by any miracle or madness a slave did get their hands on money they would not be able to do anything with it.

Laws were proposed and subsequently enacted in order to prevent access to any cultural benefits, banking, and business help that was given to whites.

Slaves were forced to work for free, as such, they didn't receive wages, so taskmasters felt they had no need of money. Because they didn't have need of money they didn't need the services that money could buy.

Laws were passed to prevent slaves from learning, which meant that since it was against the law to read they had no need of books.

Laws were passed to prevent slaves from earning, which meant that they could not be paid for working in the cotton fields or in the plantation homes.

Laws were passed to prevent slaves from attending school, which meant that they were not given the ability to learn about their local surroundings or the global world.

Laws were passed to prevent slaves from owning homes, which meant that they would be forced to always live in the shanty or outhouses they were allowed to squat in.

Laws were passed to prevent slaves from leaving the plantation, which meant they were forced to remain with whoever owned them.

Laws were passed to prevent slaves from borrowing money from banks, which technically meant they could never legally own or operate a business.

These are just a few of the laws that were placed on the books when slavery was just beginning, and they were ratified when the Emancipation Proclamation freed slaves, as a way to keep free black people in the same condition as the slaves were in.

Many of these practices are still taking place today. Institutional racism still exists to keep black people out of certain schools, housing, banking, and the glass ceiling exists in many other facets of society such as Wall Street to prevent black people from climbing the economic ladder to success.

I learned in high school economics class that incorporating and publicly selling shares in your company is the way white people create wealth for themselves, their cronies and their families, and how they kept blacks poor.

HOPE AND ANECDOTES

+ **Forgive** those who trespass against you so that you can also be forgiven.
+ **Forge** new ground, new pathways, new businesses, new relationships.
+ **Fashion** new ideas, new products, new commodities, new networks.
+ **Forget** not where we come from but rather focus on where we are going.
+ **Force** each other to be accountable to one another inside our village.
+ **Free** our minds through learning and re-education by using the library.
+ **Fret** not thyself because of evil doers because they will soon be cut off.

What can be done to reverse the reality that laws were passed to prevent black people from being part of the society?

Without resources, access to resources, or the ability to create your own resources, when the law prohibits you from doing so, limits black people from being part of the society, meaning that we have no authority to create wealth for ourselves.

I also learned in high school economics class that equity in real estate and mortgages was another way that white people create wealth for themselves and is the reason why they passed laws to prevent us from owning homes.

So many things have been done against black people from the top down that it's almost impossible to look at it all and not get a headache. It's mind boggling at the staggering amount of effort racist white people have gone through and continue to go through to keep black people down and out and in a state of poverty.

We've been allowed to climb out through athletics, acting, and other avenues that provide white people entertainment, but when it comes to leveling the playing field in areas such as education, housing, medicine, stocks and bonds, banking and a host of other economic income streams, the field is still largely white and will most likely stay that way.

Overcoming Oppression in America

Explain to Me Why You Keep Me From Participating in Society?

MAKE IT ILLEGAL FOR THEM TO LEARN OR EARN

Cash rules our society. The wealthy have the power to make an impact in their lives and in the lives of their families for generations. White Americans have had this resource and have benefitted from it for centuries. Black people still to this day in 2016, have not been able to generate wealth at the levels that white people have and never will.

Don't mention the black billionaires because there are only a handful. According to a March 1, 2016 Forbes article, out of the 1,180 in the world, only 12 of them are black, and not all of them are American. Let me put it this way, whites represent 99%, blacks make up 1%, does that make it easier to digest?

Laws were passed in America during slavery and upheld even after slaves were freed, to keep black people from learning and from earning. It is no secret that the United States National Guard had to stand in front of an educational institution with weapons drawn simply to protect black children while attending school.

So why do you think white Americans fight so diligently to keep blacks from learning and from earning?

Fortune 500 is a list of the largest companies in America. In 2015, only five black executives were serving as CEO's of the titans. Again, with 1%. Overall, only fifteen black executives have ever been at the helm of those corporations.

In the sports world, there are ninety two teams across three leagues, and as of 2015, only one black principal owner. While many black media moguls have begun to buy shares within the teams, there is still only one black owner.

The disparity of wealth in American has always been one-sided. Blacks are just now in 2016, fifty years after the Civil Rights Movement starting to gain any ground, and this will be reality for the next three to four generations.

The disparity exists because from the beginning of the country, whites stole the country from Native Americans and continue to profit from it today. Real estate started the wealth gap, but was soon met in parallel by industry, manufacturing, and stocks.

Black people are starting to make an impact and have semi-control and ownership over:

+ Higher Education Institutions

+ Films and Filmmaking

+ Hair Salons and Grooming Products

+ Clothing and Apparel Manufacturing

+ Food Franchise Ownership

Where black people still have not made much of an impact is in the areas:

+ Grocery or Convenience Stores

+ Technology Products and Software

+ Retail Mall Ownership

What is most ironic is that a vast majority of white men with hundreds of millions to billions of dollars seem to have kept the plantation mentality and have opted for black wives instead of white ones.

The reverse is true for black men with millions of dollars, as the vast majority of them seem to have joined the plantation mentality and opted for the once taboo white wife instead of black ones.

These two dynamics are at the opposite ends of each other but make perfect sense in that during slavery white men were killed for marrying black women, and black men were killed for simply speaking to white women.

HOPE AND ANECDOTES

- **Equality** emerges when all doors to wealth and wisdom are opened.
- **Equity** is the lifeblood of ownership in real estate and the road to riches.
- **Evolution** placed us 400 years behind but we had to start somewhere.
- **Energy** and exercise of our minds is how we get and remain effective.
- **Entrepreneurship** is a proven technique to use to wrangle wealth.
- **Elevation** only happens starting on the bottom & working our way up.
- **Earning** a dollar at a time is wise but it will not make you wealthy.

What can be done to reverse the reality that laws were passed to keep blacks from learning and earning?

Real Estate, Stocks, and Retirement portfolios are still the primary source of wealth in white America according to Bloomberg, Brookings, and Forbes.

It will take Black people another three to four generations to catch up to where white Americans are today, meaning we will always be at least 300 to 400 years behind.

Yes, progress is happening, and we have grown in wealth in comparison to the days of slavery, the timeline of the Civil Rights Movement, and the scope of the black family achieving the American dream.

Our steps are headed in the right direction, although the battle is still uphill. We are to this day fighting discrimination in many areas of life and most likely always will.

I look back at the history and pictures from three to four generations before us and the same protest signs being carried back then are still being carried today. We're still marching on Washington, we're still protesting black people being killed by white officials, we're still crying tears over the fact that we have to work ten times as hard to make ends meet than white people.

Overcoming Oppression in America

Wealth is Wrangled in Washington and Wall Street

CREATE ORGANIZATIONS THAT PROMOTE OPPRESSION

Klu Klux Klan is an American white supremacy focused organization that has been labeled as being responsible for much of the oppression against black people since the times of slavery.

The group held cross burnings, public lynchings, and many other dark and destructive events that are deemed responsible for causing the lives of many black people in America.

Such organizations are founded with the purpose of keeping the white race superior over other races, and it has been said that the Klan hates every race except its own and does everything it can systematically and institutionally to help ensure that all other races are prohibited access to anything that the members of the group have control over.

The Klan is not the only such organization in America. Members of other groups have appeared publicly on talk shows to voice their opinions, and have held rallies, parades, and other events to recruit as many like-minded people as they can.

Other organizations include the Aryans, Skinheads, Rednecks, Neo-Nazis, and a host of other groups. The vast majority of these groups provide white people with a way to hide their activities and actions against black people and other races, and more often than not are never held responsible for any hate or supremacy crimes they commit.

These groups have been active since the early colonization of America, but some of the more quiet and most dangerous groups are those that white men are members of that we never hear much about. Those that exist at the highest levels of government, country clubs, law, banking, chambers of commerce, and a wide variety of other industries.

They are the most dangerous because they don't wear the traditional white hoods and robes like many of the other groups do, they wear business suits and do more damage institutionally and systematically than the others.

Their philosophy is based on wealth rather than race. They exist to keep themselves, their cronies and colleagues who are members at the top of the financial chain, and they are purposed and pledged to do any and everything they can to keep their foot on the necks of black people and anyone in any other races that they feel are a threat to their way of life.

These are the groups known for their ability to blacklist people, make them disappear without a trace, and use other tactics with resources that only they have access to via their members.

Other organizations that promote oppression include those in organized crime that uses murder and fear to keep their business interests afloat.

Living in a country where white men at the highest levels of our society cannot be trusted and even those at the lowest levels of our society cannot be trusted, makes for an absolutely awful situation.

I cannot imagine living in a world where racism, hatred and oppression does not exist. Where equality is top priority, and equal opportunity is a real part of the society, rather than just a topic of discussion for forums.

I cannot imagine living in a world where discrimination has never existed. Where people can apply for and get hired based on their qualifications and character rather than their credit report and social media accounts.

I cannot imagine living in a world where property owners with rentals are prohibited from excluding people based on race, creed, color, sexual preference, or their credit reports.

I cannot imagine living in a world where people treat each other with love, respect, kindness, forgiveness, understanding, and have a heart to help rather than hurt.

I cannot imagine living in a world where slavery and incarceration are not a commodity for those who use it to uphold the laws and ways of oppression.

I cannot imagine living in such a world because it will never exist on Earth.

HOPE AND ANECDOTES

+ **Organize** people who are willing to peacefully stand up for their rights.
+ **Observe** the patterns & plans of racists in order to come against them.
+ **Outlast** oppressive policies and laws in order to work to defeat them.
+ **Outvote** bigoted agendas and campaigns in all sorts of elections.
+ **Outwit** hate driven individuals and groups by thinking steps ahead.
+ **Outshine** hatred with love, joy, peace, kindness and forgiveness.
+ **Outperform** racists at every level so that you win each and every race.

What can be done to reverse the reality that organizations that promote white supremacy still exist?

On the surface, racial hatred in America is based on the color of black people's skin. I have always wondered about how could racists be so ignorant as to hate someone because of the way they are born.

As I grew older I began to listen to racist rhetoric and in doing so I learned how narrow minded they really are. It wasn't until I began to closely watch them when they were espousing sayings such as *white power* and *keeping the white race pure* that I finally realized how misinformed they are.

If you examine the DNA of any person born on this planet you will find that no one, not a single individual, is 100% anything. None of us are 100% black or 100% white or 100% Hispanic or 100% native American.

Early in the Bible, races began mixing with other races, in places on the planet where they all looked alike, such as Palestine and Israel. And if you go to India you'll see that most of them all look alike but there are so many different cultures within their culture that you would be surprised that even they have racial hatred there.

Racism and oppression is simply stupid and I can't apologize for saying it.

Overcoming Oppression in America

CHAPTER RECAP

+ Did the previous chapter teach you something?
+ Were you moved to want to want to help in some way?
+ Do you see any possible solutions to this issue?
+ Did these facts give you better understanding?
+ Does the hope suggested below offer apt solutions?
+ Share Comments: @WhiteHatredBlackHope

HATRED
Call Them Names So They Know You Hate Them

HOPE
Praying for people's hearts to change is one of the most effective ways that it happens. Speak life to them even when they spit hate towards you.

HATRED
Pass Laws to Prevent Access to Any Resources

HOPE
Facing the reality that the majority of black people will always be four generations behind economically is one place to start dealing with reality.

HATRED
Make it Illegal For Them to Learn or Earn

HOPE
I cannot stress enough how vitally important it is for people with a passion for helping things get better in America to run for office, to vote, and to hold our elected officials accountable when they are elected to represent us.

HATRED
Create Organizations That Promote Oppression

HOPE
Dr. King proved to the world that in order to begin tearing down walls of wickedness we simply have to be willing to stand up to it face to face.

CHAPTER FIVE

CREATE DISCRIMINATORY POLICIES AND PROCEDURES

Responsibility comes at every level we grow to in life. It is often said, that the bigger the blessing the greater the responsibility. Once we know that, we are responsible for what we do with it and how we deal with it.

White people colonized America, and as such they are duly responsible for each and everything that has happened within it from the day it was incorporated as a nation.

Within that responsibility are various levels of leadership and different decisions that have to be made along the way. For example, if you are the head of a company that manufactures a product, and you need to hire workers to help produce that product, you need people both in production as well as in management.

What has happened in America is that the people in leadership positions historically, have made it so that all the power remains with them so that they are the only ones who benefit. They create and manage policies and procedures that include them and their cronies, and at the same time excludes everyone else, especially black people.

Laws were passed to keep black people in slavery and submission.

Policies were used to lock away people as punishment for refusing to work.

Procedures were set in place for how to deal with unruly workers.

Within the government many of these same laws still exist in different forms today. Within numerous corporations in America such policies and procedures still exist just in different forms.

As I write this book, it's 2016, just a few months away from the end of the year, and it's sad to think that a book like this still has to be written because not much has changed on top of the ladder, in the middle, and certainly not at the bottom.

Lawsuits are filed on a regular basis in this country claiming discrimination. People are mistreated in all facts of society and in nearly every area such as:

+ Restaurants and Service
+ Public Transportation
+ Public and Private Companies
+ Hotels and Hospitality
+ Airline Industry
+ Hospitals and Clinics
+ Headstart and Daycare
+ Elementary Schools
+ Junior and Senior High Schools
+ Colleges and Universities
+ Sports Teams
+ Railroads and Trains
+ Filmmaking and Television
+ Travel and Vacations

Discrimination exists everywhere. What's even more surprising is that racism and hatred even exists within the private homes of families. I've learned during research that some marriages where people love each other, but one spouse is of one race and the other spouse is of another race, that when they get into arguments and disagree over something, race almost always finds a way to insert itself into the war.

Dating relationships are not much different. When two people of different cultures are seeing each other and they get into an argument, before they realize it, someone has said something derogatory to the other person about their race.

The responsibility sits with each and every one of us in leadership, and the level of love we bring to the position we are in for the people we oversee can make all the difference in the world in how we treat them.

Bottom line, white people with hatred in their hearts have really messed this country up and there is a lot of work that needs to be done to repair the damage that their hatred has caused.

HOPE AND ANECDOTES

- **Make** it your mission to help put an end to racism, hatred and oppression.
- **Meet** other people where they are not where you think they should be.
- **Measure** the character of person with something other than your eyes.
- **Mitigate** all issues with fairness rather than using one-sided policies.
- **Mold** and shape your children to love people no matter their color.
- **Mourn** with the families when black people are killed without cause.
- **Motivate** others with your good works so they will see it and reciprocate.

---

*What can be done to reverse the reality
that racist policies and procedures keep oppression alive?*

If you're reading this page and are in a position of leadership in this country, regardless of whether you're the CEO of a fortune 500 company or the supervisor on an assembly line packaging pencils and pens, you are in a position to stop racism and oppression in its tracks or let it use you as a pathway to keep hurting people.

If you choose the hurting people route instead of the stop it in its tracks road I've said a prayer for your heart to change. If you're one of the people who are fed up and tired of seeing the damage that white people with hatred in their hearts does to this country and people living in this society, let me applaud you for making the decision to do what is right instead of what is white.

*Racism cannot live without a racist.
Hatred cannot exist without a host.
Oppression cannot survive without an outlet.*

Let's work together to put an end to hatred and oppression of people simply because of the color of their skin. That has gone on far too long in America and it truly needs to come to an end before it's too late for all of us, because some day, the hatred of some white folks may just piss off the wrong people.

Overcoming Oppression in America

Hire and Supervise Based on Performance Not Prejudice

POST SIGNS TO REMIND THEM THEY'RE NOT WELCOME

Imagine you were a black person and you got up tomorrow morning, showered as usual, started coffee, got dressed, got into your car and stopped at a fast food restaurant to grab a quick breakfast but once you made it up to the drive-thru menu, you noticed a sign with the letters that read *WHITES ONLY*. And when you try to place your order, instead of hearing *may I help you*, you hear *your kind is not welcome here*.

Disappointed and in disbelief, you drive away, still hungry, so you stop at the convenience store nearby. You park at the pump, being sure to get gas so you won't have to do it on the way to your kid's game later, but the moment you get out of the car and reach to push your credit card into the slot, you see another sign. This sign is similar to the one at the restaurant and it also says *WHITES ONLY*.

What would you do? This is America, you live here, you're a citizen, and you think someone has to be playing a joke. You look around but there are no cameras, and you finally notice that you're not the only person seeing the signs. There are other black people just like you, standing with the same shocked look on their faces.

You think, this isn't funny. This is 2016, who would do such a thing? Unfortunately, it is 2016, and although the signs are no longer visible in 'most' places, the same discrimination still exists in the hearts of many people and at many places that we take for granted are going to serve us because we have jobs, money, and are able to buy the services they sell.

I so wish this were true, but sadly it isn't. I've been places where I was treated as if I was supposed to read the sign. I've been places where I was treated as if I wasn't supposed to be there. I've been places where they made absolutely no point of hiding that they did not want me or my family there.

Yes it's 2016, but unfortunately the signs are still there, you just can't see them. They exist in the hearts and on the faces and in the attitudes of the people.

As a personal of color, as a black man, as a husband of over 30 years, a dad of two daughters 31 and 26, and four grand-kids ranging in ages from 10 years down to 2 years, I'm always on the lookout for anything that can cause harm to me or to my family.

I'm never confused about the reason why *my kind* may not be welcome in some establishments. I've even had this experience in some of the oddest of places such as the public library; the bathroom at a travel stop; in the line waiting to get on a ride in an amusement park, and so on. Shopping malls are the worst.

I've managed to teach myself how to ignore people but it is very difficult to do given that I'm a Pastor, always ready to share God's love with any and everyone who is ready to receive it.

The signs that black people, my ancestors, and even some of my family members have been forced to live with, endure, and face over the past 50 plus years of my life, and long before I was born, are still as degrading today as they were back then, even if they are no longer publicly hanging where we can see them.

It is absolutely ridiculous to know that we are 16 years into the millennium and we are still having to face the looks, snarls, stares, be followed around in many stores, and be treated as if our money is no good in certain outlets.

We are a resilient people. Black people are by nature a resilient people. We come from a history of living amongst lions, tigers, hyenas, snakes, rhinos, and other wild animals, so a human being that doesn't kill us, simply makes us stronger. And even when you do kill us, and certainly you've darn sure killed a lot of us, it has also made us that much stronger.

White hatred fuels black hope. I'll say it again, without white hatred, many blacks wouldn't have the reasons we now have to hope that things will be better for us in the end. As Christians, like so many of us are, we believe that in the end, hate filled white people are going to be punished in a manner that we as black people couldn't possibly muster up the power to even push out. We believe that it's part of the blessing we receive for our forgiveness.

HOPE AND ANECDOTES

- **Believe** that things can be better then help work to make it happen.
- **Break** through all ignorance by hanging welcome signs in your window.
- **Branch** out and share your love with others so love grows and grows.
- **Bless** people of all races, creed, color, sexual orientation, when you can.
- **Burn** signs in your mind when you see them so they don't affect you.
- **Burst** out and laugh when you see signs of hate so it won't anger you.
- **Be** the one to always take the high road and leave hate beneath you.

---

*What can be done to reverse the reality
of publicly posted and hidden agenda signs that promote hate?*

Hatred hurts. It's one of the worst things I've ever had to deal with in my life. I grew up in the sixties, so I saw the actual television reports on the news of people being sprayed with water hoses, having dogs turned on them, the national guard having to be called just so people could attend school.

I've seen the tears that so many mothers cry because their babies were killed and dads who will never get to raise their sons because of white people who hate. I've seen news of blacks forced to move out of their homes because they were burned down from a Molotov cocktail thrown in their window.

Hatred hurts. The fact that white people refuse to stop this madness lets me know that we have to simply fight that much harder today in 2016 than Dr. King and thousands of others did in 1968. We have to take the fight in new directions, and work to ensure that the hidden agendas of hate can no longer be publicly or privately displayed on the walls or in the hearts and on the faces of the people we interact with.

Hatred hurts. There is no sign that can fix it. There is no magic potion that can heal it. It has to start in the heart. I often wish this were a bad dream that all black people would one day wake up from, but sadly, it is all to real.

Overcoming Oppression in America

Closing Doors and Posting Signs Can Exclude The Best Person For the Job

CHARGE CONVICT & IMPRISON THEM ON FALSE CHARGES

All my life I've been accused of things I didn't do. It wasn't long after I turned five years old that I was accused by a sibling for doing something that I knew one of my other siblings had done. Even when they found out the truth behind it all, I was never exonerated or apologized to.

In more recent times I've had officials in charge of my life after prison look me in the eye during a conversation and tell me that they teach officers how to write criminal complaints to help ensure people are convicted. "The more charges you pile on, the more likely you are to get them to plea to something."

As I sat there listening, you would think that I would have been in disbelief and shock but I wasn't because I've known most of my life how hateful white men do things. All I could think about was 'but you say I'm the criminal!?'

White people have been accusing, charging, convicting and imprisoning black people on false charges for centuries. We should not expect it to stop just because the Emancipation Proclamation and the Civil Rights Movement paved the way for us to finally participate in this society.

The reality is that we live in a country where many white Americans want black people dead or in servitude. It is unfortunate that the tactics that officials and accusers use are still responsible for so many black people being incarcerated today.

Things are supposed to get better, but all slavery did was move inside an institution, it never actually stopped. All the Civil Rights Movement did was force white people with hatred in their hearts to find other ways to oppress and abuse us.

White people know that black people with felonies carry a stigma that comes along with a set of branded paint brushes that cause a stain that most often can never be removed. They set up systems and operate behind closed doors to help ensure that we are constantly reminded that they have the power to do just about anything they want to us without recourse.

We are seeing more evidence of it just because nearly everyone has cell phones with cameras on them, but we've lived with this fact our entire lives.

Camera on cell phones and the fallacy of police body cameras that they can conveniently switch off, is simply another way to placate the public and make people seem as if they aren't really witnessing what they are seeing.

Police brutality has existed since slavery. It has only progressively gotten better because some white people's hearts have changed as a result of getting to know black people and learning that we are not the pariahs their parents and grandparents told them we are.

What recourse do black people have when we are accused, charged, convicted, and imprisoned on false charges? Absolutely none. It is rare for anything to happen as a result of or retroactively when the truth finally comes out about a black person being screwed by people in the system who are simply doing their jobs to help put another black person in prison.

There is no recourse for legal actions taken against a black person who has no resources to hire attorneys to fight and seek justice for their situation.

There is no recourse for such action when the very people who are paid to protect and serve are the ones who commit the crimes against you to begin with. Their word against yours is likely to always turn out against you.

The word 'justice' carries another title with it in the black community, which is 'just us'. For black people we know that means justice is not for us. White people know it to mean justice is designed to protect them, and hang us.

In the conversation I was having with the officials in charge of my life after prison, while the tone was cordial, they were laughing and joking, and the mood in the room was that of respect, but I knew that they were dead serious about what they were telling me.

This glimpse and insight into the tactics used for centuries against black people within the law, justice and prison system is something I thank them for because it helps me to pray for God to have mercy on their souls.

HOPE AND ANECDOTES

- **Statistics** prove and history shows black people wrongfully convicted.
- **Swallow** your pride and anger in order to forgive those who abuse you.
- **Shout** to yourself the words *I'M FREE* even if you're incarcerated.
- **Strategize** on how to keep your focus away from revenge at all times.
- **Soar** above your circumstances no matter what situation you're in.
- **Stay** prayed up and peaceful, so you will be content in your circumstance.
- **Strip** away the stigma layer by layer until you are free to function again.

---

*What can be done to reverse the reality
that false charges on criminal complaints is still used as an abuse of power?*

White people with hatred in their hearts have used false charges, criminal complaints layered with trumped up charges, lies, planted evidence, and all kinds of abuse of power to help keep black people in chains.

Each and every time I look back at the centuries we have been enduring their hatred and fighting the battle, the only thing I can come up with as a reason behind it all is that this is our cross to bear.

Black people know that the meek shall inherit the Earth. We know that greed and selfishness are on the way out, to make way for God and salvation. We know that while white people who hate us were trying to find ways to conquer us, we learned that we are more than conquerors.

White hatred fuels black hope because it is the one thing that they cannot take from us. They have killed generations of our families, stolen centuries of our years, kept us impoverished, uneducated, and incarcerated.

We learned to be content in our condition because there is a God and He sees what we go through and hears our cries for help. Every season must change, it is time for white hatred to step aside so black hope can step up.

Overcoming Oppression in America

RUIN THEIR REPUTATION WITH FALSE REPORTS

Your good name is a thing the Bible says is better to be chosen than even great riches. You can lose wealth but still have the ability to get it back again, but once you lose your good name, almost no one will trust you enough to want to help you again.

I've been there. I've unknowingly, and most often unintentionally, burned many bridges in my life. What I didn't know at the time is that those bridges were attached to my good name, which became bad literally overnight.

Although I've made some decisions that caused harm to my own name, I've also experienced where officials in authority and people who think they have power, have done damage to my reputation by abusing their power and spreading false reports about me and my character.

Overcoming a bad reputation starts with being honest with yourself about the fact that it exists and facing the reality that the only way to restore your good name, reputation, and make progress in your life is to forge another pathway that is not in any way related to the reason(s) behind a bad name.

Black people have been living under the hatred of some white people for centuries. That hatred often includes having them tell their family, friends, colleagues and cronies not to have anything to do with you. They will often lie and say that you've done something that you didn't, abusing their power and causing harm to your reputation.

There's no way to stop people from calling around to everyone you know, or every person you meet, or anyone you try and do business with. Sure you could gather evidence that it's happening, and people could tell you that once you left their home or place of business that someone called to spread untrue gossip about you. But fighting it should not be your focus because people tend to believe what they hear, regardless of whether or not it is true.

You'd be fighting a losing battle the moment you start wasting your time, energy and effort to try and stop people from lying on you behind your back.

The best way I've learned to deal with this when white people with hatred in their hearts have done it to me, and it has happened numerous times, and I could have easily turned over the evidence I gathered and that which people gave to me to the authorities for them to look into it, but it is not a crime to slander someone, and trying to sue wouldn't necessarily solve the problem.

The problem is that those who lie on you in an attempt to ruin your reputation know that people have a tendency to believe what others say about you. It's a natural thing to want to hear gossip about someone. Television and reality shows have made it an industry all unto itself.

But what I've learned is the best way to battle this abuse of power and lying behind your back is to move forward, in spite of people trying to make it be an obstacle in your path.

You have to go down a new path, plant your feet firmly in that place and space and pray to God to have mercy on the souls of the people who are working diligently to ruin your reputation.

White people with hatred in their hearts against black people have done this more times than could ever be recorded. And because ones good name is more valuable than riches, they know that once you lose it, that it is most difficult and next to impossible to get back.

When people try and sabotage any and everything you try to accomplish by working to ruin your reputation you have to do your absolute best to not respond to it. You have to leave it and them in God's hands, let Him fight the battle, and walk away believing that He will.

Jesus never did anything wrong when He was down here in human form. Yet people today still mistrust Him because of all the things people with hatred in their hearts did to try and ruin His reputation. And the way Jesus responded to it is exactly the lesson we need to learn in order to deal with it the same way He did, which is to ignore it. The battle for your reputation is not yours to fight. You cannot stop people from telling lies on you, spreading untrue gossip about you, or even telling people about your background, or something they think you did. What you have to do, is something new.

HOPE AND ANECDOTES

- **Resilience** is standing your ground in spite of what others do to you.
- **Rejection** is part of being black. Keep knocking until a door opens.
- **Refuse** to give up no matter how badly hateful people treat you.
- **Refer** to testimony of others who overcame what you're going through.
- **Read** the Bible for strength, stamina, endurance and longsuffering.
- **Revenge** is for people who want to become like those who oppress you.
- **Repair** damage to your reputation if you can, if not, keep moving forward.

---

*What can be done to reverse the reality
of the damage a bad reputation can do and people who lie to others about you?*

Technology has given white people with hatred in their hearts against black people the ability to continue to be cowardly, take the hoods of their heads, come out from behind the robes, and sit in the comfort of their homes and offices and damage your reputation.

All the things they do against black people in secret have been done for centuries so don't be surprised that this is just a new way for them to continue doing what they've always done.

Having a new method is not going to stop their madness. You cannot fight a battle against an enemy you cannot see. What's done in the dark will eventually be exposed to the light.

Your focus should be on consistently doing good so that any lies they tell people about you being bad will eventually be overtaken, overshadowed, and overwhelmed by the tremendous amount of good you've doing, instead of the bad they lie and say you've done.

Forge a new path, do good things, and let God fight the battle against the enemy that you can't see, because they cannot hide from Him.

CHAPTER RECAP

+ Did the previous chapter teach you something?
+ Were you moved to want to want to help in some way?
+ Do you see any possible solutions to this issue?
+ Did these facts give you better understanding?
+ Does the hope suggested below offer apt solutions?
+ Share Comments: @WhiteHatredBlackHope

HATRED
Create Discriminatory Policies and Procedures

HOPE
If you're in a position of leadership as CEO, manager, supervisor, or even lawmaker, with the authority to change discriminatory practices, do so.

HATRED
Post Signs to Remind Them They Are Not Welcome

HOPE
Hatred can be displayed in many forms. One of the most common ways of the past was *whites only* signs. You can help change this with a *welcome* sign.

HATRED
Charge Convict and Imprison Them on False Charges

HOPE
If you know of, are aware of, or are in a position to help right the wrongs being done to people when they are charged with a crime that has numerous other unrelated offenses attached to it, step up and say something about it.

HATRED
Ruin Their Reputation With False Reports

HOPE
When someone wants to ruin your reputation they can hide behind technology, but everything done in the dark will get exposed by light.

CHAPTER SIX

REFUSE TO COMPLY WITH THE PROCLAMATION

The Pharaoh we are fighting today is different than what people had to fight in the past, but the hardness of their hearts are very similar. In the past, even when the slaves were set free, the Pharaoh of that time went back on his word and called his army to arms and set out to kill all the people he had just set free.

The same is true today. It's a different time but the same circumstance. The Pharaoh of today knows that the Emancipation Proclamation is the law, but he has called his people to arms and they have never stopped killing the slaves and descendents of the slaves they once set free.

The anger behind the slaves being freed back then hardened the heart of the Pharaoh in Biblical times, and it has hardened the heart of the Pharaoh in today's modern times.

Maybe you've heard it explained this way:

An object in motion stays in motion unless acted upon by an unbalanced force.

Slavery has continued since Biblical times, the only thing that has changed is the Pharaoh and the motion or method in which it is being carried out.

This quote by Newton doesn't say come against slavery with the same motion, it says act upon it with an unbalanced motion. This means that black people have to do something that is so unheard of, out of character, unthinkable, and *'unbalanced'* against the laws of nature that it will seem foreign to the motion and movement of slavery and thereby stop it in its tracks.

Let's examine what such an unbalanced force could be:

+ **Unity**
White people and people of other races are fighting alongside black people and although it makes a noise, the overall impact has not stopped slavery.

+ Prayer
God already knows about slavery. It was Him that hardened Pharaoh's heart. Mentioning slavery to God is not the unbalanced force needed to stop slavery. 'Mentioning' is not a motion or a movement.

+ Proclamation
The law has been on the books since 1865 but it hasn't stopped slavery.

+ Inclusion
Black people are being included in many areas of life but it hasn't stopped the slaughter of innocent black people.

What I believe is the unbalanced force needed to stop slavery in its tracks is for everyone on the planet who is willing to stand up against slavery to FAST and PRAY together.

We've been praying about this issue for centuries and nothing has stopped the motion of slavery against those who are oppressed by it. The only thing that has **never been done** in the history of slavery is for millions of people, coming together to Fast and Pray. If we ever hope to put an end to slavery:

We have to work to **change the balance of power**
from white hatred to black hope.

We have to **change the balance of power**
and meet hatred head on with love.

We have to **change the balance of power**
by denying our flesh to end being dehumanized.

We have to **change the balance of power**
by coming together against their wicked ways,
so God will hear from Heaven and heal our land.

I firmly believe the unbalanced force that has been missing all these many centuries, is for all the people who want slavery to end to come together on one accord, with Fasting and Prayer.

HOPE AND ANECDOTES

- **Trust** in God is the most important weapon in the war against racism.
- **Torture** can't win over non-violence protests and standing up for rights.
- **Treat** everyone with honor and respect even if they don't deserve it.
- **Think** of others more highly than yourself & teach kids to do the same.
- **Treasure** everyone you know as if they are pure gold and diamonds.
- **Take** time to inform the younger generation about the past history.
- **Teach** the truth no matter how damaging and hurtful it is to set us free.

---

*What can be done to reverse the reality
that refusal to honor freedom from slavery is still causing oppression?*

With all the laws passed, nonprofit organizations in place, and an all out effort to end oppression taking root over the past several centuries from protesting, you would think that we'd be much further along by now.

The problem is that white people with hatred in their hearts still oppose the freedom black people received behind slavery; they oppose the casinos and sovereign nation status that Native Americans received behind losing their land. And even though the laws have changed, and there are countless people working to put an end to the bigotry, the powers that be at the top, are still in power, still in control, and still have hatred in their hearts.

Black people are a resilient people. We've endured so much over several centuries that we have learned to deal with it in our own way, even when white people go so far as to take the lives of our children for no reason other than taking their long-standing hatred out on us.

I'm keenly aware of the hidden agendas and the ways that people who hate are using technology to continue opposing the laws and the efforts of people who have been working to put an end to oppression for generations and you should be aware too.

Overcoming Oppression in America

We Are Now Fighting Briefcases, Business Suits, and Badges

DENY THEM LOANS FOR HOUSING OR BUSINESSES

In today's society it would seem innocuous for a black family to get denied a mortgage based on their credit or lack thereof; collateral or lack thereof; or just their overall financial package not meeting the basic criteria and standards for underwriting approval.

And though this seems to be the case in a lot of housing applications, given the economic crash of 2008, we now know that white men have been playing around with people's lives and financial well being in this arena as well.

There are news reports all over the country where people have lost their homes to foreclosure because their monthly mortgage tripled and or the value of the house became less than what was owed on it. I'm still shocked and appalled at the fact that there weren't tens of thousands if not millions of white folks going to jail for many years behind this issue. I'm not surprised that the public was given a couple of fall guys who took the fall for everyone else on the team.

As a result of this gargantuan theft against hard-working Americans there are former homeowners of all races now living in tents and campers and many are now totally homeless behind this crisis.

The travesty is that the banks and mortgage companies received billions in bailout money, but homeowners were left holding the bag, losing their homes in the process, behind the very banks and mortgage companies that wrote bad loans on them in the first place.

This injustice is just a glimpse into what black people have been dealing with all of our lives. We've been denied housing based on the color of our skin; unable to live in certain neighborhoods and forced to live in ghettos and housing projects in order to keep certain areas of the country *white only*.

The economic crash behind the mortgage crisis was a wake up call to the rest of the country about the greed and selfishness of white men in America although I really don't think many people were paying attention.

Black people have suffered for centuries under the same financial brick wall of being denied loans simply to start businesses while corporate crooks such as Enron, thieves such as Madoff and Petters, state senators such as the S & L Keating Five and a host of others are able to take billions from the American people only to end up with most of the people involved receiving a slap on the wrist in lieu of a fall guy taking the brunt of the blame.

For centuries black people have been denied the ability to participate in the stock market at a level that would benefit our broader community.

For centuries black people have been blocked from raising investment capital from venture capital firms that would benefit our broader community.

For centuries black people have been prohibited from buying in to the chain and retail store franchise marketplace that would benefit our broader community.

For centuries black people have been closed off to the approval of commercial bank loans to start manufacturing products that would benefit our broader community.

For centuries black people have been mistreated and forced to stand by and watch the wealth of white people continue to grow while we become poorer and poorer by the day.

For centuries black people have been specifically targeted by white people who would deny our applications for housing, loans, investment, and all forms and types of assistance.

What white people would approve for black people however, is public assistance, or welfare. If you cut off avenues to employment, prevent access to loans and mortgages, the only thing left for black people to do is head down to the welfare office where white intake counselors would be waiting with open arms.

We've seen the damage greed in white people has done to this country's economy. If we keep going in the same direction, things will only get worse.

HOPE AND ANECDOTES

- **Cash** is king in this society and black people have been kept from it.
- **Corporate** colleagues have helped one another get and stay on top.
- **Collaboration** across multiple industries kept black people out.
- **Collectors** have benefitted from items black people have never owned.
- **Cushioning** the blow with welfare is a slap in the face to black people.
- **Catalysts** like nonprofits were created to respond to greed & need.
- **Coins** trickle down to black people in the form of Affirmative Action.

What can be done to reverse the reality that black people continue to suffer because of being denied access to wealth?

The scales of financial wealth for families has been unbalanced for centuries. White people have benefitted in immeasurable ways while black people have been forced to suffer under the weight of it all.

As mentioned in an earlier chapter, it would take another four generations, or four to five hundred years for black people to catch up to white people in the areas of wealth, which is to say it will never happen.

Black people were blocked from being a part of this society in any kind of positive and productive way, from the very beginning of this country. We were prohibited, prevented, and passed over, for everything.

It is a travesty to now see the incredible talent and creativity in black people today who are making a slight impact and taking great strides to show the world what we are capable of, knowing how many of our ancestors had the same talent and capability and were never given the opportunity or the option to utilize it.

White people need to step up and correct this injustice and they need to make sure it gets done long before the next five hundred years go by.

Overcoming Oppression in America

Cash is King in this Society and Black People Have Been Kept From It

STEAL THEIR INVENTIONS, PRODUCTS & PLANS

Patents are pieces of paper that show others what you have planned and put together. If you're the inventor of a better mouse trap, in order to manufacture it, you must patent it so you can protect it, first. The problem is that during slavery, after slavery, and long since slavery, white people have stolen the patents, products and plans of many black people.

I've mentioned throughout this book that history shows that what white people cannot conquer or control, they find a way to steal and profit from it.

According to several sources, The Patent Act of 1793 and 1836 prohibited slaves from obtaining patents because they were not considered citizens.

According to Bloomberg.com, in 1861, Jefferson Davis, president of the Confederate States of America, enacted a patent law that allowed enslaved black people to receive patent protection for their inventions. Nine years later in 1870, the U.S. Government passed a patent law giving all Americans, including black people, the right to their inventions.

Because as history shows us all too often, even when black people attempted to patent their inventions, they were blocked by the patent office.

Many of the inventions of black people have made life easier for the masses but the black families of the inventors never profited from them. Today, many of those inventions are claimed and controlled by white Americans who profit greatly and generationally from them.

There are numerous books, blogs, articles, and bibliography on this subject, what the inventions are, who was responsible for them, and who was subsequently able to benefit from them so I won't bother preparing a list.

My intent is to show that black people often created products out of need, to solve a problem or to make a process better, but the greed of white people has always been right there to either claim, conquer, or control that which they had absolutely nothing to do with.

Other tactics used by white Americans in order to propel themselves into the space of a product that is being invented is the strategy to make it a corporate policy that anyone who works for a company and during tenure with that company, invents a product, the company is entitled to a share or all of said product.

The product could be totally unrelated to the company but because the employee worked there while it was invented, the company can often claim part ownership.

There have been and still continue to be many lawsuits arising out of patent and trademark disputes. However, typically when black people are involved the balance of power steps in and the black person almost never wins.

History has shown us that black people's contribution to this society have been largely ignored, denied, and swept under the rug, instead of celebrated for their brilliance.

It has been said that necessity is the mother of invention, and it would certainly serve to reason that because black people had more needs than anyone on the planet since America began, that we would be the creators and catalysts for many things that would make our lives better.

Many black inventors are credited or partly credited with inventing or improving upon products such as the toilet, traffic light, cotton gin, gas mask, shoe lasting, and so on, but during the times we lived in when those products were produced, and the patents subsequently filed, black people rarely had the opportunity to reap the rewards.

In modern America, things aren't much different. Black artists, record producers, song writers, inventors, manufacturers, and others, often see their products and inventions being duplicated by white Americans as if they were the first to create or launch it.

For example, as recent as 2015, a lawsuit went forward claiming that the music to one of the world's most famous songs written by a black man, was used as the beat and background to a recent song, which earned millions.

HOPE AND ANECDOTES

- **Inventions** are supposed to benefit the inventor. Work to make it so.
- **Innovation** ignites, inspires, increases, and should also include blacks.
- **Inspire** all people to make like better for all not just white Americans.
- **Ignite** our youth by showing them black people's contributions.
- **Improve** processes and products for the masses and re-patent them.
- **Incorporate** with others so you always have a team approach.
- **Include** our elders in the process so they can pass on their wisdom.

What can be done to reverse the reality that black people's inventions, products, and plans have been stolen or denied?

Given the level at which we're seeing black people emerge and showcase our talent and ability it serves to reason that out of all the books ever written on black inventors and their contribution to society, it is a travesty that there are only a handful of us actually recognized. Some of the most amazing black people have never been adequately lauded for their role in making live better for the masses. We could browse across several industries and see black people at the top of their game doing some absolutely incredible things in their respective arenas, but for the most part, we are still in the early stages and the infancy of what is to come.

Black people own TV and radio networks, film studios, record companies, pro sports teams, are top actors and actresses, pro sports players, recording artists, and every position you can imagine from astronaut to zookeeper, talk show and game show hosts, authors, inventors, and news anchors. We've advanced because we're finally able to showcase talent that white people with hatred in their hearts, wished we would never have been able to share with the world. Other black people are waiting to emerge from the shadows, to show that even though our ancestors were treated inhumanely, and that treatment still exists today, we are a resilient people who deserve to be recognized for our contributions, and not ridiculed for our color.

Overcoming Oppression in America

Black people's contribution to society have been largely ignored, denied, and swept under the rug, instead of celebrated for their brilliance.

KILL THEM WHEN THEY PROTEST

Victory can only be achieved if you're raising your voice. In America, the First Amendment grants people the right to free speech, and to peaceably assemble. As history shows us, the only way to engage masses of people in a process to improve it is to protest.

History has also shown us that when black people are at the helm of such demonstrations, our leaders have been assassinated. As recent as 2016, one of the leaders of a movement protesting the killing of innocent black people by police officers was found shot to death and burned in his car.

Social Media has served as the conduit and is used as a platform for voicing our opinions and for gathering groups of people together at a specific place and time.

Cameras on our telephones and smart devices have provided what seems to be indisputable evidence that inhumane treatment of black people is still taking place all over the country by white people with hatred in their hearts.

If you could dig the dirt from over Dr. King's grave and tell him of the modernized version of the Civil Rights Movement, he would probably say in surprise, "It's 2016, and it is still taking place?"

The fact that we are still seeing black leaders having to risk their lives to stand on the front line against injustice is still as appalling today as it was during Dr. King's time.

This year has produced not one but two employee strikes by nurses against their employer; pilots against their airline employer; technology and other communication workers against their employer, and so on. But I have not heard of one report of anyone in any of these protests losing their lives because of their refusal to be treated just any kind of way.

Black people seem to be the only group in America that is constantly and consistently killed for raising our voice in protest of bigotry and hatred.

This is crystal clear evidence that racism is still alive in America, and black people are still on the ground with white power's foot on our necks.

Such injustice should not be taking place given the vastness of this land and the amnesty received for enslaving black people.

Wasn't stealing the land from Native Americans and enslaving black people enough?

Such injustice should not be taking place given the centuries of control.

Wasn't forming and running the government for centuries enough?

Such injustice should not be taking place given the immeasurable amounts of wealth they've had and poverty we've had.

Wasn't having it all and owning all the wealth for centuries enough?

Such injustice should not be taking place given the millions of our black ancestors killed without the murderers ever being prosecuted.

Wasn't immunity from prosecution for genocide enough?

What will it take for white people in America who still have hatred in their hearts to learn to love everyone for who we are and stop focusing on the color of black people's skin?

What will it take for white people in America who still have hatred in their hearts to learn to accept all people regardless of their race or religion?

What will it take for white people in America who still have hatred in their hearts to learn to love someone other than themselves?

Why are we still seeing reports of black people and our leaders losing their lives over raising their voice in protest of the fact that **white people don't own this planet**, we all live here! OMG! This is utterly ridiculous in 2016! White people do not own this planet, but I believe if they could they would. And they would take away gravity from under everyone but themselves.

HOPE AND ANECDOTES

+ **Love** crushes hate, conquers color, embraces excellence, in all people.
+ **Leadership** should not be a prerequisite for murderers or martyrs.
+ **Life** is a gift from God and no man should have the ability to return it.
+ **Leveraging** assets should include value black people bring to the table.
+ **Loss** prepares for gain, but will blacks see a return for our sacrifices.
+ **Litmus** is a moral test that black people aced centuries ago.
+ **Losing** loved ones hurts, but blacks believe in healing and forgiveness.

What can be done to reverse the reality that black people are still being killed for stepping up as leaders against hate?

Suppressing someone's words when they could be wise enough to have the solution to a long-standing problem is a travesty that takes place in America all too often.

Dr. King's speeches provided many Americans a platform to listen to and get behind a vision for a better reality. His voice echoed the sentiments of people who otherwise had no opportunity to speak.

The rhetoric of hatred continues to plague black people in this country. We have yet to live a single year without seeing a hate or supremacy crime profiled on the screens of the nightly news.

Centuries of oppression are still being logged into the databases of census records and the outcomes are still primarily unbalanced toward the benefit of white Americans. This is no longer a *whites only* society. White Americans are slowly becoming the minority, which may be the primary reason many of them are still fighting so hard to keep their status and position in society. What they don't realize is that it would take centuries more to move them from the top of the tier because of all the damage they've done and continue to do in numerous facets of life in America.

Overcoming Oppression in America

CHAPTER RECAP

+ Did the previous chapter teach you something?
+ Were you moved to want to want to help in some way?
+ Do you see any possible solutions to this issue?
+ Did these facts give you better understanding?
+ Does the hope suggested below offer apt solutions?
+ Share Comments: @WhiteHatredBlackHope

HATRED
Refuse to Comply With the Proclamation

HOPE
The law made slavery illegal, but the people made it last. We can continue to work against bigotry and bias until it no longer exists in our society.

HATRED
Deny Them Loans For Housing and Businesses

HOPE
Keeping black people down by denying them access to resources, simply prevented white Americans from seeing how valuable black folk really are.

HATRED
Steal Their Inventions, Products, and Plans

HOPE
The United States government needs to do more to officially honor the contributions of black people. Until that happens, white Americans will continue to believe blacks have no place or part in America.

HATRED
Kill Them When They Protest

HOPE
It's 2016, and black people are still being killed for standing up for what is right. If we diligently prosecute those who kill it may serve as a deterrent.

CHAPTER SEVEN

CONTROL LAWYERS & JUDGES TO GET CONVICTIONS

Bribery has been a long-standing method of being able to control the prosecutorial process and ensure convictions. Black people have suffered under this miscarriage of justice for centuries.

Throughout the history of slavery and oppression, when a black man spoke to a white woman, all she had to do was say she felt threatened, and the black man was either charged, tried and convicted, and sent to prison, or hanged.

There have been many cases where white women didn't even have to say anything about being spoken to. If there were white men present who witnessed a black man look at a white woman, black men were charged, tried and convicted, and sent to prison, or hanged.

This injustice continued well into the 1960s and remnants of it still exist even today in spite of the fact that there are countless biracial couples and marriages all over the country and throughout the world.

Bribery has been one source to control prosecution of black people, threat has been another. If there were white men or women confused about wanting to stand up for the rights of black people, other white people would call them N-Lovers, make threats to them and their families, until they were absolutely clear on what they were supposed to do the black person.

Bribery was one, threats was another, murder was used as a last resort. Many white Americans gave and lost their lives trying to help black people escape prosecution and hanging.

White people stood on the front lines against injustice right along side black people. Many were lawyers, judges, politicians, clerks, bailiffs, and even some police officers. Sadly, those who refused to comply with the threats and accept bribes to ensure prosecution of black people were murdered along with the blacks they were trying to help. White Americans with hatred in their hearts have a history so dark and demented that one wonders if there can ever be any hope that things will change. That wonder is always escalated when black people are killed for no apparent reason by police officers with hatred in their hearts, but they are never prosecuted or even lose their jobs.

Lawyers and Judges are often the last line of defense for black people against trumped up charges, being falsely accused, and facing wrongful conviction. The system of public defenders itself is a joke in that their paychecks come from the budget of most prosecuting attorneys offices.

Bias, bigotry, and bribes, have a long history of being the norm in the criminal justice system in America. I really believe that black people thought that when a black President was elected that things would change, but in reality we should not be expecting anything to change for the better as long as there are white people with hatred in their hearts still alive in America.

No black President, or even if the next 43 Presidents were black people, nothing would change in this country with respect to who is in control of the criminal justice system.

The systemic injustice that exists in law enforcement and the judicial system has and always will be largely based on slavery. This model and mentality has and always will be primarily the reason for much of the corruption that exists within the system.

When you can have a black man and white man go before a prosecutor and get charged with the exact same crime; then go before a judge with the exact same plea deal; statistics show that a very large percentage of the outcomes end up with probation for the white man, and an extended prison sentence for the black man.

Miscarriages of justice within the system when one of their own is charged with a crime is even more difficult to prosecute. In the past few years, when black youth and black men, and even a few black women were killed and there were officers or officials involved, only 1% of the crimes were prosecuted, and an even lower percentage of those that reached a courtroom ended up in convictions. Being acquitted is the white man's get out of jail free card.

HOPE AND ANECDOTES

+ **Justify** all charges and convictions through an unbiased process.
+ **Juries** should hear all the evidence not just what is picked by judges.
+ **Justice** can only happen if the officials involved in it are unbiased.
+ **Jails** are full of black people there behind excessive and false charges.
+ **Judicial** process should never be in the hands of secret grand juries.
+ **Join** in the fight against judicial corruption to bring justice to everyone.
+ **Jesus** Christ was falsely accused, convicted, sentenced & murdered.

What can be done to reverse the reality that black people still suffer under the decisions of corrupt officials?

Prosecutors have too much power as a single individual in the criminal justice system. The court system is littered with situations where without prosecutorial misconduct, many individuals would never get charged.

I rarely if ever watch crime shows on television, because I typically maintain control over what I feed my spirit, and the images I allow to enter my mind, but when I do allow myself to sit and watch one of these shows, I always see situations where the prosecutors are devising schemes to get convictions.

All prosecutors are not culpable, and there are many great, noble, honorable, and honest prosecutors all across the country, and they should be applauded for the work they do and the difficult decisions they often have to make.

However, when a prosecutor is part of the long-standing system that has hatred as its mission statement, oppression as its protocol, and locking away black people as its campaign, I strongly believe that miscarriages of justice occur far too often. The fight to remove these people from their offices, and provide the public with unbiased individuals who will do their jobs without being controlled is difficult and may never happen in this society as long as bribery, threats, and murder is used as tool to keep them in office.

Overcoming Oppression in America

Miscarriages of Justice Still Exist and Black People are Still the Target

PREVENT EARNING A LIVING UPON RELEASE FROM JAIL

Every time I've been arrested and taken to jail not to return home for six months at a time, I've had a home and wife and kids and family to return to. My wife, now retired after 20 years as a teacher and director of a nonprofit, is an early childhood educator who was able to maintain the level of living we're accustomed to even while I was incarcerated.

This is extremely rare for most black men being released from prison. Most men who are incarcerated do not have the benefit of such comfort when they are released from prison. I know all too well that my wife and my life are both very rare commodities as a black man with a criminal record.

Another way white people with hatred in their hearts keep demonizing black people with felonies is through the use of sabotage and other tactics. Some of those other post-release tactics and strategies include:

+ Passing laws to make it nearly impossible for felons to find housing.

+ Making it legal for landlords to discriminate against applicants.

+ Make it difficult for employers to hire people with criminal convictions.

If a person can't get stable housing after being released from prison, everything else in their life that depends on that housing is likely to fail.

If a person can't find employment to pay for housing after being released from prison, everything else in their life that depends on that income is likely to fail.

I am a living witness to the sabotage and strategies and tactics that officials can use against a felon once they are released from prison. I'll consider writing the book to share my testimony and release the evidence at some point in the distant future, but it's not important to me perse, but I know the information will be invaluable to help not only prosecute those involved, but to also help those who like me, have been affected by this kind of hatred.

Earning a living upon release from jail is paramount to being successful post incarceration and to help avoid becoming a part of the staggering statistics of recidivism.

The criminal justice system is a business. If there are no criminals to arrest, charge, prosecute, sentence, and jail, the system would shut down. Jails are a business. Without inmates they would shut down, so everyone involved in the judicial system, intentionally and unintentionally work to help keep people incarcerated and the system working and paying their salaries.

Historically, black people have been maligned and mistreated by the criminal justice system and many of the officials that work for the system for centuries. We are not surprised when it happens or why it happens or who causes it to happen. We are fully aware that it most likely will happen.

I believe there has been a master plan in place to prevent black men from being the head of our homes, leaders in our church, respected in our communities, and able to effect change in our country.

Felons often lose their family.
Without the black man as the head of the house in a traditional two parent family, that family often suffers undue hardship for many years during and after that period of incarceration.

Felons cannot vote or run for public office.
Passing laws to prevent felons from being able to vote is another way white people with hatred in their hearts keep black people from participating and effecting change in the political and judicial process in this country.

Felons are subject to being rearrested for violating release terms.
Yet another way to keep a foot on the neck of a person who has been incarcerated, this is an often used method of disrupting the life of that person especially when the person is black.

The criminal justice system, which has been biased and targeting black people since its inception, needs to be completely overhauled or the statistics and the destructive effects on the lives of black people will never get better.

HOPE AND ANECDOTES

- **Government** is responsible for the plight of many people post prison.
- **Gather** all the skills you can & use your gifts & talents where you can.
- **Grace** is rarely used in post-prison decisions but it should be used often.
- **Greed** is the primary reason for wanting to keep black people in prison.
- **Groups** exist that can help ex-offenders reintegrate into society.
- **Gain** ground by knocking on every door you can until one opens.
- **Goals** are never met until and unless steps are taken to meet them.

What can be done to reverse the reality that black people have been commodities for the judicial system for centuries?

The unfair challenges that black people still have to face being released from prison is a blatant and targeted attempt at taking away our dignity, pride, and passion.

When you prevent a black man from earning a living to support his family he feels less than a man, and I believe that is exactly what white people with hatred in their hearts intend.

I feel this way because I'm reminded of the signs that black men held up in protest during the Civil Rights Movement which read *I AM A MAN*. Because we were treated like we were not human, we were not considered citizens.

We are human and we are citizens. The past 50 years have proven that we not only have the ability to do some incredible things, our earning potential is just as high as anyone else.

We are gifted beyond even our wildest imagination and given a chance and the opportunity to showcase our God-given gifts, we can bring more to the table than most anyone and can be a benefit to just about any company, project, or organization, from line staff to management to executives.

Overcoming Oppression in America

Recidivism is a Business and Businesses Without Clients Close

MAKE IT LEGAL FOR LANDLORDS TO DISCRIMINATE

Every man, woman, boy, girl, and family, deserves a decent and safe place to live regardless of whether or not they are a felon or have a criminal record. Lawmakers have passed laws that place a stigma on the lives, credit reports, and criminal records of people who have been incarcerated.

This is a completely unfair disadvantage that keeps some incredibly skilled people from being hired in positions they are more than qualified for, and instead keeps them in jobs that are menial at best.

White people with hatred in their hearts know how difficult it is for black people with a criminal record to find housing in this country because that is the way they intended and planned for it to happen.

The NIMBY (Not In My Back Yard) SYNDROME is one that has been used against black people in every area of society since the beginning of slavery in this country.

They are of the mindset that it's OK for black people to slave and serve, but it is not considered OK for us to live next door, attend the same schools as white kids, or work anywhere close to where whites work.

Landlords have been discriminating against black people for centuries. We were prohibited by law from obtaining mortgages, and once that was found to be illegal, and the law was eventually and subsequently changed, more battles to add laws to the books that continued to oppress and suppress black people ensued.

These battles are still being fought, even as recently as a 2015 victory to ban the box that asks whether a job applicant or housing applicant has a criminal record.

It is always best to be up front and honest about your background but people don't want to be excluded from being considered on the basis of a mistake.

Everyone one this planet sins, and we've all made bad decisions, make mistakes, and have done some things we absolutely regret.

These oversights and errors in judgment should not be the decision-making component for denying people stable housing. Not everyone has an 800 credit score and the truth of the matter is that some of the people who are allowed to rent homes and apartments have worse records and credit scores than those who are denied the opportunity.

Black people have been denied such opportunities based on the color of our skin since we were enslaved and brought to this country. Add in the false charges of a crime, a conviction, and a criminal record, and we become the pariahs that white people with hatred in their hearts already want us to be.

On paper, in credit reports and background searches, black people are much less likely to be approved for housing, than any other people group. Even people who are immigrant have a better chance than black citizens.

Allowing landlords to discriminate against applicants and primarily target black people is unjust and probably illegal. It is yet another way to keep oppressing black people and it needs to be stopped.

It's ridiculous to think that white people with hatred in their hearts would be happy if black families all lived in ghettos, tent cities, homeless shelters, and in places far away from where whites live.

It's ridiculous to think that just because people are black that the property values will decline when we move into a neighborhood.

It's ridiculous to think that black people do not maintain and upkeep their residences any less than our white neighbors.

It's ridiculous to think that when black people are ready to move, that we're going to steal every appliance, door, light bulb, and anything else not nailed down.

These are some asinine notions that many landlords honestly believe.

HOPE AND ANECDOTES

+ **Work** diligently to dispel myths about black people and housing..
+ **Wait** patiently for perceptions to change but continuously advocate.
+ **Walk** in your communities so that people will know you and yours.
+ **Welcome** neighbors during annual events such as national night out.
+ **Witnessing** oppression should compel you to want to help stop it.
+ **Whites** are historically fearful of black people for no real reason at all.
+ **Wisdom** knowledge and understanding can go a long way in this battle.

---

*What can be done to reverse the reality
that landlords discriminate against black people based on laws and myths?*

I've owned numerous rental properties in my lifetime. I'm quite familiar with the process of placing an ad, interviewing potential tenants, accepting applications, and screening those documents for possible hazards and red flags so that one can work to weed out any unforeseen problems.

The problem with the process is that even when you are a black person and the owner of rental property, because of what our ancestors went through and our own experiences have taught us, and what our kids will likely face in their lives as well, we should look to abandon the litmus test of sorts and simply make a decision based on whatever criteria we use for determining who we select as a tenant.

I've also had the experience of helping to manage rental property owned by a church. One would think that the church would be more compassionate with those who were in need of housing, and especially in situations where they could not pass a credit or background check. I won't go into detail but I witnessed worse circumstances in this context.

Helping to eliminate barriers to stable housing is vitally important because landlords actually support segregation when they choose to discriminate.

Overcoming Oppression in America

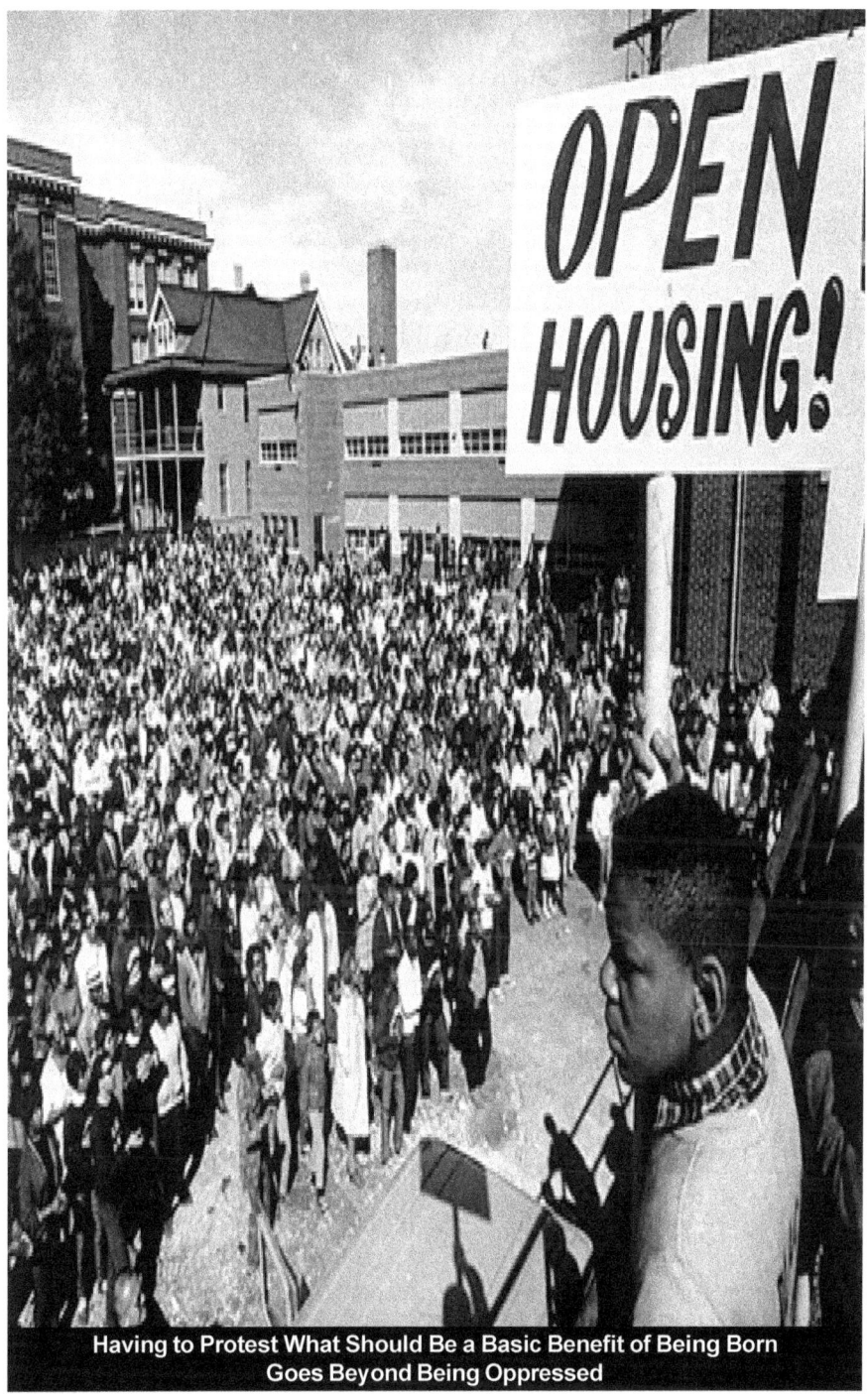

Having to Protest What Should Be a Basic Benefit of Being Born Goes Beyond Being Oppressed

MAKE IT DIFFICULT FOR EMPLOYERS TO HIRE

Employers should be able to hire who they want when they want and how they want. This would be an ideal scenario that could better serve the American society irrespective of who were members of the population.

Since the beginning of slavery blacks have been burdened under the tactics and targeted bigotry that says if you're black you can't work certain places; if you're black and a felon you need not apply. Many people never face the reality and truth that if I wasn't black I probably wouldn't be a felon.

Laws, unwritten rules, policies and procedures make it difficult and next to impossible for employers to receive any benefit or breaks from the government for hiring black applicants who have been maligned by the madness.

Employers have acclimated to the national agenda that says its OK to be biased against black people when they come in your place of business looking to apply for open positions.

Black applicants have proven to be much more effective and efficient at their jobs in many cases, but because of the stigmas placed on us because of color, class, credit, and crime, we are at a disadvantage before even walking in the door.

Many employers have adopted the status symbol of promoting themselves as *Equal Opportunity Employers* though the executives, managers, supervisors and other overseers of the internal corporate policies and protocols tell a vastly different story.

In a recent interview on a PBS talk show hosted by a black man, I listened to the testimony of another black man who stated that his being a felon has placed him in undue financial hardship, and his claims of being forced out after ninety day stints of working temp and other positions have become commonplace in his life and endeavor to find gainful, lasting, living wage employment to care for his family.

I mentioned in an earlier chapter that white people with hatred in their hearts and who are in positions of decision making at places where people want to work, often continue the old habits of oppression and prohibit black people from earning a decent enough wage to support their families.

Many pockets of protest are popping up all over the country, such as those in Seattle and Minneapolis seeking to increase the minimum wage for workers up to fifteen dollars.

This may seem to be a stretch to make it happen state by state and certainly those in power at the federal level have taken a back seat, don't ask don't tell stand on the issue.

Workers are worthy of their wages, and while it is up to employers to set their wages according to the national standards, those standards have been biased and based on bigotry from the beginning.

This keeps the old adage *The Rich Get Richer* alive and well on the backs of the poor and most often black people.

New national standards for salary and stipend need to be adopted in order to enable all workers to support themselves and their families.

New rules need to be integrated that follow the model of allowing employers to make their own hiring decisions regardless of a person's color, class, credit, and criminal history.

New norms need to be developed that give employees and employers benefits for reaching certain benchmarks.

Increasing the minimum wage will definitely provide a modicum of relief to employees but what is additionally effective long-term are incentives to stop shipping American jobs overseas where the workers are willing to earn less for manufacturing and producing American products.

Trade relations is indeed a valuable way to maintain better business relationships with other nations, but not worth it at the expense of our jobs.

HOPE AND ANECDOTES

- **Newness** comes when old ways are no longer setting the precedent..
- **Nothing** keeps bigotry alive except whites with hatred in their hearts.
- **New** policies should always benefit today and tomorrow's Americans.
- **NAFTA** was intended to benefit all countries inside the agreement.
- **National** standards should improve the lives of citizens not burden them.
- **Never** put your life in the hands of any person who wants to end it.
- **Nobility** is earned doing good, not by being rewarded for being racist.

---

*What can be done to reverse the reality
that employers following national standard for hiring is keeping oppression alive?*

The national standards for hiring has placed even more burden on black people. While we have constantly throughout our lives and the lives of our ancestors been discriminated against because of the color of our skin, and the class we have been identified by, but only in the past fifty years (which I believe is in direct opposition and response to the Civil Rights Movement), have employers begun using credit and crime as criteria for consideration.

This new normal has tipped the scales against black people even further away from equality and have made even more of us question how we get from under this gauntlet, and will we ever be truly free?

Answers to these and more poignant questions simply serve as reminders that we live in a nation with people who have hatred in their hearts for black people and they want us either dead or in servitude.

Their rules and regulations, policies and procedures, laws and localities, have been and continue to benefit white America with no regard for black life, black history, black contribution, or black culture.

We are in 2016, but the mindset makes it seem as if we are still in 1776.

Overcoming Oppression in America

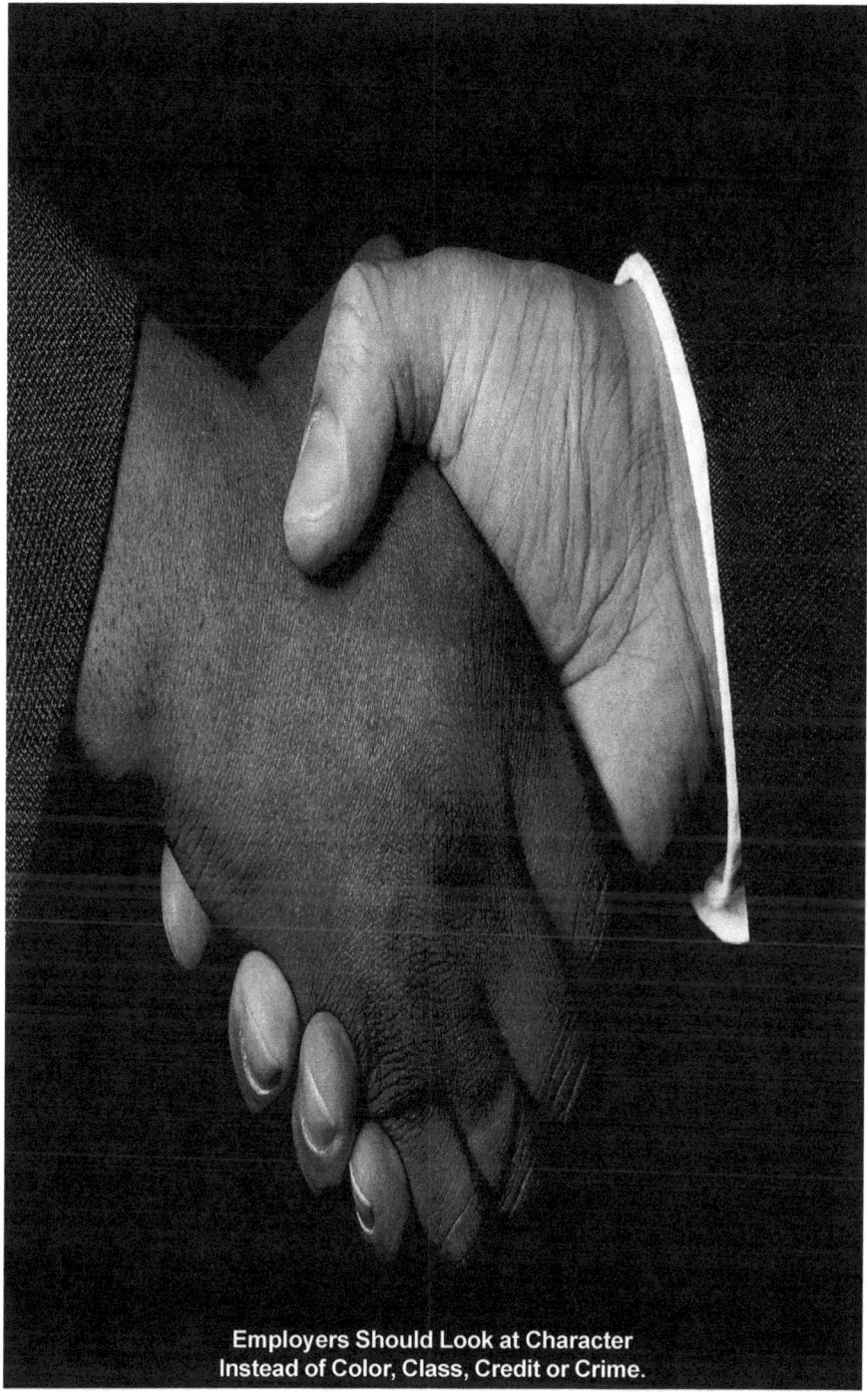

CHAPTER RECAP

+ Did the previous chapter teach you something?
+ Were you moved to want to want to help in some way?
+ Do you see any possible solutions to this issue?
+ Did these facts give you better understanding?
+ Does the hope suggested below offer apt solutions?
+ Share Comments: @WhiteHatredBlackHope

HATRED
Control Lawyers and Judges to Get Convictions

HOPE
Stop the process within the judicial system that allows prosecutors and judges to gamble with people's lives without regard for a fair trial.

HATRED
Prevent Earning a Living Upon Release From Jail

HOPE
The mindset and motivation of recidivism continues because it is a business and without clients businesses close. Give people options and opportunity.

HATRED
Make it Legal for Landlords to Discriminate

HOPE
Without stable housing everything else suffers. The fight for equal housing has been at the forefront of American life since the country was incorporated. Broader penalties need to be in place for landlords who discriminate.

HATRED
Make it Difficult for Employers to Hire

HOPE
Elimination of national criteria based on color, class, credit, and crime so employers can make hiring decisions based on character.

CHAPTER EIGHT

GIVE THEM GUNS DRUGS AND ALCOHOL BUT NO JOBS

Englewood is the neighborhood in Chicago where I was raised. I was proud to live there, attend elementary and junior high there, play four sports there, serve as captain of those sports teams there, was president of the student council there, loss both my parents there, and I have relatives and lifelong friends who still live there.

Englewood is the place where the vast majority of the gang related crime happened back in the sixties and seventies when I was coming up, and it is still holding on to that statistic today. I left the community in 1983, went to work for a company that had national accounts to I was able to travel, and I eventually got married, settled down, and move out of Chicago in 1991 when I relocated my family to Minnesota.

While in Englewood, I witnessed firsthand how guns, drugs, and alcohol was used as a way to set a course in the master plan of white Americans with hatred in their hearts for black people that we would never recover from.

Keeping black people intoxicated and inebriated and incarcerated and addicted and unemployed was part of their master plan.

This was and still is a targeted effort by hateful white people who I believe hoped black people in such communities all over the country would commit genocide on ourselves using the guns they dumped into our communities.

I am a living witness that white men would stop freight trains on the tracks inside our community, open the rail cars, get in their cars and drive away. Inside the rail cars were crates and crates of guns and ammunition.

I am a living witness that white men would bring cars full of marijuana and cocaine into our community, get out, open up the trunk and get into another car and drive away.

I witnessed both of these activities on numerous occasions. It started and funded a way of life we came to know of gangs, guns, drugs, alcohol, & jail.

When the city approves more liquor stores inside a community than they do churches, factories, and jobs, there is a targeted effort to keep the people living in that community in poverty. When the police refuse to answer the calls and cries of the parents inside a community to come and help they are trying to stand back and let the people in that community kill themselves.

Although the master plan of hateful white Americans worked, it didn't have to. I make absolutely no excuses for the fact that the young black men in our neighborhood who took guns and ammo from those rail cars and drugs from the trunks did so. We certainly did not have to. But when you have no jobs, your parents are struggling, and suddenly you see a possible way out, at the time it looked like a blessing, but it was indeed a cruel curse.

+

Where do unemployed drug addicted people who cannot afford to pay for their drug of choice, get the money to buy their high? *They steal it.*

+

What do unemployed drug and alcohol addicted people do with free guns and ammunition? *They turn on each other.*

+

What do unemployed drug and alcohol addicted gang members with free guns and ammunition do when they have no hope? *They kill each other.*

+

What happens to all these people when they wake up from their drug and alcohol induced states and begin to recognize what has happened to them? *They awaken to the reality of a criminal record, unemployment, and homeless status.*

Most people in my community never woke up. Many were killed by cops; others died in their addiction; some are still there feeding their high each and every single day since I escaped. I believe my escape is part of the reason I'm such a target today. I wasn't supposed to survive. But I did everything I could to stay alive to be able to tell the story of how it all started.

I'm grateful and thankful I was able to get out and pull my family with me.

HOPE AND ANECDOTES

+ **Keys** to happiness in a society is when all citizens are able to benefit.
+ **Kites** can fly high and far away if there is no string holding them down.
+ **Killers** use various methods of ending someone's life, I know that now.
+ **Killing** black people for sport gave many white Americans gold medals.
+ **Kindness** is the foundation of every relationship, but it is not black reality.
+ **Kingdoms** can only stand when every citizen is able to participate.
+ **Knowledge** of your enemy is effective when used to elevate each other.

What can be done to reverse the reality that keeping black people intoxicated, inebriated, addicted, unemployed & incarcerated is a master plan.

As someone who survived Englewood I believe that instead of systemic incarceration, militarizing young black gang members can help channel their anger and also aid in maturing them into men. It can also engage them in real battles, and can serve as a pathway to integrate them into society as responsible citizens.

There are countless success stories of young black men who believe they never would have made it out of the ghettos they were living in without enrolling in higher education institutions or enlisting in the military. **The military, affords them the opportunity to do both.**

95% of the people I grew up with are either dead, incarcerated, or addicted. There's not much difference today. The guns are bigger, drugs are stronger, jail sentences are longer.

I don't know why Englewood became such a target in someone's master plan to eliminate the black people who live there, but it certainly was and is. The results are seen today as a seemingly never-ending cycle of drug and alcohol addiction, guns, crime, killing, and jail. Someone needs to locate and interview the train engineers and vehicle transporters from back then.

Overcoming Oppression in America

One Can Take Down a Thousand - Two Call Fell Ten Thousand.

HAVE MEDIA & FILMMAKERS PORTRAY THEM NEGATIVELY

Headlines in newspapers and lead stories on the nightly news all over the country has for a long time been slanted and biased against black people. As a former news reporter, I wrote feature articles on many subjects.

As a filmmaker with over 100 short films produced, and one feature film script written and currently in production, I understand the responsibility the media and filmmakers have when portraying people in the proper light.

Fantasy coming out of Hollywood is one thing, but the angle of the premise and the story line can either make people think about black people in a positive or negative way.

There is an incredible burden that black men carry as the head of our household. We are supposed to be good providers, great dads, incredible husbands, and phenomenal leaders in our church and respected in our broader community.

When a black man cannot fulfill these tasks, internally we feel less than a man. Our black male ancestors took to the streets in protest of their inhumane treatment by carrying signs that read *I AM A MAN*.

While everyone can easily see that a man is a man, my dad, his dad, and many of the men in their family who joined others in protest of bigotry and hatred coming from white people with hatred in their hearts, did so because they were fed up with being treated like something less than human.

The media and filmmakers have continued from the past to today, using negative portrayals of black people to keep white supremacy alive and well in all aspects of American life.

While black face is no longer the norm other methods and means of keeping such images at the forefront of people's minds are still being used today. Racist ads, commercials, and news stories are continuously being published and aired across networks and national news stations all over the country.

In the history of American filmmaking, the award for being acknowledged by your peers in the industry has been taking place in the form of the Academy Awards, which first began in 1929.

In the 87 year history of the ceremony, amongst the 2,947 awards that have been given to actors and actresses, only 18 black people have ever reached the top tier.

Let me put this into perspective:

2,929
Oscars given to white actors and actresses.

18
Oscars given to black actors and actresses.

This is the type of biased and bigoted business that white people have been doing for centuries. This is called *balance* to them but to us, it's business as usual.

This staggering statistic simply brings to light the long-standing and continued blacklisting and bigotry that takes place in many industries.

Media and Filmmaking are interesting industries. They both are tasked with the duties of entertaining people with everything from sitcoms to talk shows to nightly news to feature films. And while black people are typically the subjects of and are used in a vast majority of these productions, history shows that rewarding us for our roles or participation is still in the dark ages.

When I first researched this section and came across these statistics I had to get up out of my office chair, walk across the room and sit in the comfy captain's chair, and sink down into it's cushion just to soften the blow. I'm a black man so I wasn't shocked or surprised at the numbers, what hit me is that it has been and is still so biased and blatant that my mouth is still open.

HOPE AND ANECDOTES

- **Quit** participating in biased activities that do not include all races.
- **Quiet** voices cannot be heard; be vocal to let others know of problems.
- **Quick** methods of reaching the masses include social media groups.
- **Quiz** yourself and your family and friends to see if you have prejudice.
- **Quilts** are a fantastic way to remember contributions of black people.
- **Qualms** are expected when you are nervous, but speak out anyway.
- **Quirks** are natural feelings, being treated inhumanely is not.

What can be done to reverse the reality that portraying black people negatively in film and media is intentional?

+

Have you ever seen news stories of white gang members portrayed on the nightly news? When was the last time?

+

Have you ever seen news stories of black gang members portrayed on the nightly news? When was the last time?

+

Does this give you any indication that news stories are slanted to portray black people in a much more negative light than white people?

I'm still amazed by the numbers as it relates to the bias and lack of balance in the media as it relates to news reports about black people. We seem to be the only ones ever in trouble, ever killing or being killed, ever in gangs, and the only ones that white people should be afraid of. Heck, if I were a white person being fed all the images I see in the media and in films about black people, I'd be afraid too!

This has to change, but the only way it will is if all people make it happen.

It's No Secret to Black People Who's Targeted With the Lens.

KEEP KILLING ENTIRE GENERATIONS OF THEIR FAMILIES

Possibly the number one reason that many black Americans are still upset with white Americans with hatred in their hearts is that an innumerable number of our ancestors, our grandparents, parents, siblings, and children have been and are still being killed by supremacy crimes.

According to the FBI 2014 UCR's Hate Crime Statistics report, 47% of the 5,462 bias incidents occurring were based on race. These statistics further show that we still have a major problem with bigotry in America.

White people with hatred in their hearts are responsible for killing entire generations of black people in America. These numbers are staggering as well. According to the U.S. Census, more than 11,000,000 black people were killed in America prior to the turn of the century in 1900.

Considering the fact that these were primarily murder by hanging and also other crime such as gun violence and black people being burned by fire or dragged to death behind vehicles.

How do you plan to kill someone, get a group of people to witness it, hang scores of black people with nooses around their neck, then take a picture of it, and absolutely nobody gets charged with a crime?!

These blatant forms of racial injustice still continue today, in 2016, they just occur in various other forms, are hidden and not so unashamedly open.

+

Police officers kill black people at will with little to no prosecution.

+

Racists kill black people at will with little to no prosecution.

+

Cross burnings and torch burnings still occur in the U.S. with little to no prosecution.

Generations of black families were murdered with little to no prosecution. If the numbers of an estimated 11 million black people having lost their lives to racial hatred with little to no prosecution are true, it should anger you.

The TV show *How To Get Away With Murder* has the title right, just the premise is wrong.

For clarification, let me say that I'm a huge fan of Shonda Rhimes, a black woman, with incredible talent, and she should be lauded for creating such amazing work to bring to television.

White people with hatred in their hearts and any white person who has ever benefitted from what has happened to black people in American should truly be ashamed of themselves.

It is difficult for me to stomach writing about this topic at times, but I know how immeasurably important it is to continue to tell the story, share the history, and never let the memory of our ancestors, our grandparents, parents, siblings, and children, fade from our memories.

They deserve better.

Slaves stolen from their native land of Africa to pick cotton deserve better.

Native Americans deserve better.

Black people killed by white racist cops deserve better.

White people with hatred in their hearts killed off generations of black men, black women, black children, black families, just because they could.

There has been no apology, no retribution, no recourse, no reparations, and they wonder why it is still difficult for some black people to recover from our history.

Hope is the only thing many of us have to hold on to. Hope is the one thing we know you cannot take from us.

HOPE AND ANECDOTES

- **Voices** raised in unison to unite against injustice is a powerful force.
- **Vocalize** through protest and demonstrations but keep it peaceful.
- **Visit** memorials and museums to show support and to remind others.
- **Value** was placed on black people to sell into slavery with no recourse.
- **Virtue** no longer exists when you treat people as if they are not people.
- **Violation** of anyone's human and civil rights makes *all* people angry.
- **Victory** is not yet won, but will be ours when glory finally does come.

---

*What can be done to reverse the reality
that genocide in America against black people has not ended?*

Every time I hear of another news report of a black person in America losing their life to another white person with hatred in their heart, it simply sickens me to my stomach that we are still at a place in this world where white people think they have to hold on the notion that they are superior.

This fallacy, fantasy, and fictitious ideal is what fueled racial hatred in this country in its inception, and what has keep stoking the fires of injustice until this day.

It is a travesty to know that there is still little to no prosecution taking place when supremacy crimes occur.

The lives of black people in America carry no value to white Americans with hatred in their hearts and as long as this is the reality, black people will continue to be in danger.

> *Mothers are numb from crying, fed up with burying their children.
> Fathers are tired of fighting the battle of racism against humanity.*

Many black families have no more words to explain why it still happens.

Overcoming Oppression in America

Don't Pray For Me I'm Already Dead
Join Me in Praying For Those Who Killed Me Instead

SEGREGATE THEM IN ALL FACETS OF SOCIETY

It's 2016 and we're still talking about segregation. Hard to believe? Not if you look at it from this perspective: It has only been 48 years since Dr. King was assassinated. Given that I'm 53 years old, and that I was old enough to watch television news reports of the aftermath, it should help you realize that the battle for human and civil rights in America by black people has been going on far too long.

While it's not hard to believe that we're still fighting about segregation in 2016, many of us are not surprised. White Americans with hatred in their hearts have been trying to keep the following areas of this society as *whites only* for centuries. Aside from banking and venture capital firms, of which there are few black owners, and no black airline ownership, let's examine a few of the other industries and look at the progress, if any, being made.

GOVERNMENT
First black politician elected to Congress was in 1870. Although we now have numerous black elected officials their power and provision is limited. For example, in the U.S. Senate, out of 100 members, only two are black. Since 1870, only nine have been black. Of the 435 members of the U.S. House of Representatives, currently there are 46 black officials. Again, we seem to be making progress on getting the positions, but power is limited.

SCHOOLS
Brown V. Board of Education of 1954 was the benchmark for establishing what should have been a fundamental right, however in 2016, schools in communities of color are still 70% behind white schools in financial health.

SUBURBS
Home ownership by black Americans is making progress in areas once prohibited by law and targeted by teams of white real estate brokers.

EMPLOYMENT
Existing battles continue to rage on for a higher minimum wage. Breaking through glass ceilings is a big battle for both black male and female execs.

FILMMAKING
There are a handful of black producers and directors making impact in Hollywood, but in terms of studio owners, there is still a very long way to go.

ACTING
Given the 2,929 Oscars awarded to white actors, and only 18 awarded to black actors in the history of the Academy, these results say it all.

SPORTS
Out of the four major sports, which includes a combined 122 teams namely: NBA, NFL, NHL, MLB, only two of the majority owners are black. Another uphill climb & major battle ground for black people spending green money.

BROADCASTING
This is a major battle ground that is a very big problem. Inclusion into television and cable ownership has not increased much at all since the FCC implemented a 'Minority Ownership Policy' in 1970. However, a Republican led Congress in 1995, undid the policy and the progress.

REAL ESTATE SALES
As of 2015, there are still under 10 black owned major real estate companies making any impact nationally.

STOCK BROKERAGE
There are about 75 black stock brokers but research shows no black owners.

CONSTRUCTION
Black construction and real estate development continues to climb uphill but the majority of contracts and new construction is still white controlled.

RECORDING
Black artists continue to make strides in this arena, but industry decisions are still made inside the whites only boardrooms.

TECHNOLOGY
Only one major firm still continues to hold the top black owned spot in this industry, and not surprising, Silicon Valley is still considered *whites only*.

HOPE AND ANECDOTES

+ **Accept** that blacks started on the bottom and help them rise from there.
+ **Areas** where you can assist in breaking through glass ceilings, do so.
+ **Acclimate** toward industries where they are still fighting for equality.
+ **Agree** that whites are responsible for and benefit from black slavery.
+ **Argue** for fairness and equality in every facet of society until it happens.
+ **Access** avenues where blacks are still being prevented from entering.
+ **Attitude** of gratitude is the foundation and forgiveness is the force.

---

*What can be done to reverse the reality
that black people are still fighting against pockets of segregation?*

Black people are still largely segregated in America, but there is progress being made at various levels and in several sectors.

Given that wealth is and will always be an unbalanced scale there can never be any comparison between white and black financial health.

White Americans have a history of stealing lands from natives to colonize America, forming the government to enact discriminatory laws to segregate its citizens and keep themselves in power, built wealth on the backs of black people, and have held onto and maintained control of the majority of industries since its inception.

Pockets of segregation still exist in America and our need to continue the fight for both civil and human rights is still evident. In addition to keeping all the profits from free labor by enslaving black people, white Americans have always had the benefit of being able to pass long, share, and inherit stolen and slavery-based wealth, which is one of the single-most glaring reasons that black people will not catch up to white wealth for at least another four to five generations. We continue to fight and remain hopeful while living with the harm & hell of the fallout from centuries of oppression.

Technology is Another Tool Used to Torture and Taint Talent

CHAPTER RECAP

+ Did the previous chapter teach you something?
+ Were you moved to want to want to help in some way?
+ Do you see any possible solutions to this issue?
+ Did these facts give you better understanding?
+ Does the hope suggested below offer apt solutions?
+ Share Comments: @WhiteHatredBlackHope

HATRED
Give Them Guns Drugs and Alcohol But No Jobs

HOPE
Implement change by helping black people to heal from the past while providing provision, programs and services to help navigate our future.

HATRED
Have Media and Filmmakers Portray Them Negatively

HOPE
Stand against bigotry and bias while taking the fight to those industries such as broadcasting who still refuse to open up ownership to black people.

HATRED
Keep Killing Entire Generations of Their Families

HOPE
Killing black people without prosecution is the same slap in the face as slavery without freedom. This fight is about human rights and we need to put those responsible in the same jails they have held us in for centuries.

HATRED
Segregate Them in All Facets of Society

HOPE
Push aside the power; break down the barriers; strike down the signs; and do all we can to integrate every sector of society where doors are still closed.

CHAPTER NINE

WORK DILIGENTLY TO CRUSH THEIR HOPES AND DREAMS

How does one work against an entire culture of people trying to press forward toward the mark of the high calling and pave new pathways toward success? The answer is simple: close doors, block access; be biased and bigoted; and serve up constant reminders that black people are not wanted or accepted.

CLOSE DOORS
Keeping black people out of the sectors of society by closing doors in our faces takes places in many forms. Doors are still closed to executive offices in many corporations where the black talent pool is rich with applicants but the glass ceiling is in place to keep us from breaking through.

Money seems to be much darker than the standard shade of green when it is in the hands of black Americans, from the perspective of white America. We have the wealth to be able to operate and build bridges of success in the many marketplaces where we have historically been denied, though the gates are still closed and secured with chains and invisible *whites only* signs are still hanging.

Crushing the hopes and dreams of black people who are diligently pursuing the American dream of a sustainable career with ample compensation and retirement packages; home ownership with honest mortgages attached; auto, homeowner, life, and health insurance rates that are manageable; education that is both effective and energizing; and investment institutions that don't steal from their own funds.

Black people simply want the same opportunities to create wealth that any other person on the planet, without the handouts, hurt, and harm that comes along with white America opening its long closed doors to anyone but itself.

Black people have proven that we are not only resilient, but also intelligent, inspirational, intellectual, innovative, and can be instrumental in every area of society that we are allowed to operate in. We cannot continue on the path of our past, which is where see our hopes and dreams were shattered.

BLOCK ACCESS

History has proven that black people have been blocked from entering everything from government to schools. Although the National Guard has long since walked away outside from the entrances, the fight is now taking place inside the institutions where systemic injustice and the reality of racism still exists.

There are blatant miscarriages of justice taking place in every sector of society and the slap in the face is simply another way of telling us to *stay in our place.*

Before we can kick the doors down through peaceful protests another wall to block access has been raised against us. Before we can believe that we've made a breakthrough using our character and creativity another obstacle of oppression blocks an opportunity.

Although we are running the same race, and historically we have been still at the starting block while our white counterparts have lapped us century by century, we still have the same hopes and dreams as most everyone else in that we have yet to see true equality.

BE BIASED AND BIGOTED

Hatred in the hearts of white Americans has been the fuel to light the fires of frustration inside black Americans for centuries.

Other than evidences of evil, we still have yet to full understand why we have been so hated by white race and culture since we were first encountered during their explorations of other nations.

Why did you have to intrude on our lives and disrupt our way of life while we were in Africa? You could have called us savages from a distance. You could have picked your own cotton. You could have sold each other instead of us.

The bias and bigotry of white America against black Americans has gone on far too long and it is our hope and dream that white hatred will unite with black hope to banish bias and bigotry to make America beautiful and better.

HOPE AND ANECDOTES

- **Banish** bias & bigotry by breaking through barriers & building balance.
- **Bury** bias and bigotry inside businesses that still hold on to such policies.
- **Bring** every race to the table in discussions that affect all Americans.
- **Build** bridges that provide pathways to promise, prosperity & provision.
- **Believe** that united we stand and divided we most certainly will fall.
- **Bravery** and boldness is what started the fight for civil & human rights.
- **Benefits** come to everyone when everyone is allowed to be beneficial.

---

*What can be done to reverse the reality
that the hopes and dreams of black people are still crushed from the top down?*

Don't repay evil with evil, pray for those who persecute you, do unto others as you would have them do unto you, trust God and do good, are all Bible scriptures and sentiments expressed by the founders of this country. Though we have discovered, are still learning, and continue uncovering truths about many of the men & motives responsible for laying this nation's foundation.

We are not focused on the past, but rather driven with laser-like vision for the future. We understand that there have been some crushing blows dealt to Native Americans and black Americans throughout history that cannot be undone. We stand on the shoulders of all before us to avenge their deaths by making life better for everyone, not just a privileged few.

We are benefactors and beneficiaries of our destiny on Earth and strive for salvation in Heaven. We believe that confession and repentance, grace and mercy, forgiveness and understanding, topped off with a dose of love and happiness can help us heal from our past, and serve to frame our future.

The benchmarks, milestones, and outcomes we project offer us a victorious view from our side, once we break through the barriers, bias, and bigoted beliefs from where white Americans with hatred in their hearts look from.

Overcoming Oppression in America

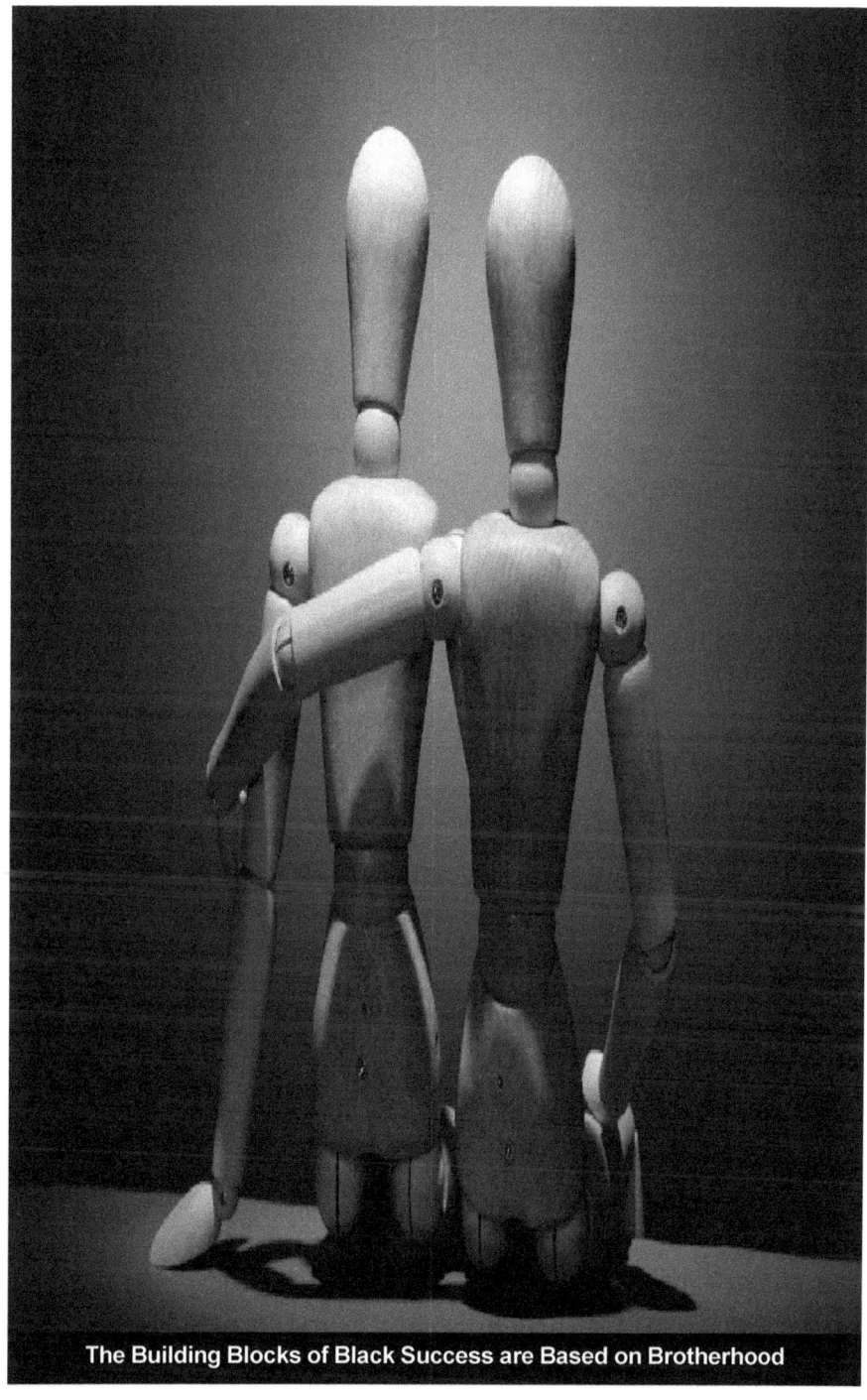

The Building Blocks of Black Success are Based on Brotherhood

SECRETLY USE THEM TO TEST DRUGS AND VIRUSES

The maniacal methods used by white Americans with hatred in their hearts include evil intentions and inventions, and have not been limited to simply slavery.

Some of the mayhem came in the form of hypodermic needles laced with all types of addictive substances, dangerous drugs, and vicious viruses. And much of it was targeted toward black people.

We are still learning of the many missions that teams of white Americans tasked with the assignment to inject black people in both America and Africa with infections intended to end the black race and control the spread of the black population. I've compiled a list of some of the most known.

SYPHILIS
According to the Centers For Disease control, in 1932 the Public Health Service began a study to justify providing treatment for black people. The 600 black men involved were told they were being tested for bad blood when they were actually being given Syphilis as guinea pigs. In 1974 an out-of-court settlement was reached.

TUBERCULOSIS
In my early years, when I was supposedly being vaccinated to protect me from certain diseases, nurses would often prick my arm. After those encounters, which seemed normal at the time, my dad, a medical professional at the time, began wondering about side effects. Before those encounters, I never had any health issues. Since then, my skin has tested positive for TB.

AIDS AND EBOLA
Many conspiracy theorists have for a long time, been convinced that similar to the government funded Tuskegee experiment on black men to test Syphilis, many believe AIDS and EBOLA are simply further attempts to find a way to eliminate significant numbers of black people and leave a virus within them that is highly contagious and will remain within the construct of the family DNA for centuries.

Given what the government did to our own Veterans with Agent Orange, and the subsequent discovery of the Syphilis experiment against black men, I believe white people with hatred in their hearts employed by the U.S. Government are highly capable of such atrocities.

PCP AND LSD
According to DrugAbuse.com, PCP was created and marketed by a government funded lab and in 1957 it was used in clinical trials on humans.

MARIJUANA
Like Nicotine, this drug is extremely addictive. White Americans are now legalizing and profiting from it, while black people are incarcerated over it.

COCAINE
Although this substance became the drug of choice for affluent white Americans, it quickly spread to the black community with targeted plans.

HEROINE
One of the most highly addictive drugs available anywhere. Once addicted, deliverance from this dangerous drug is difficult.

CRACK
Credited with the destruction of more black families than any other drug, it is still used as a weapon in the black community today.

It is my belief that evidence clearly shows the evil intentions to bring about genocide on black people on both continents. Their plans began to backfire when many white American children started experimenting with the same drugs their parents with hatred in their hearts created to use against us.

Meth and Ecstasy are two of the most prominent, but since this epidemic began, many other iterations of these substances continue to find their way into white American society with a force and fallout that hateful white people never saw coming in their own communities. This has created a panic and more secrecy amongst them that continues to be funneled through nonprofit programs and groups that offer inpatient and outpatient drug addiction and counseling services.

HOPE AND ANECDOTES

+ **Coalesce** with each other to help uncover patterns of patient testing.
+ **Cooperate** with lawyers and advocates finding evidence of experiments.
+ **Communicate** and compare stories across social media to uncover it.
+ **Challenge** the government to release information on the secret labs.
+ **Change** the laws so that people can be prosecuted and testing can stop.
+ **Counsel** each other via support groups to help start the healing process.
+ **Coordinate** national efforts to help bring this issue to the forefront.

---

*What can be done to reverse the reality
that black people have been secretly used to test drugs and viruses?*

Every time I hear the list of side effects during many drugs being advertised on television, it brings me back to reading and researching many of the news reports about blacks being secretly used to test drugs and viruses.

I can't imagine why anyone, white or black, would do this to another human being unless they absolutely have no moral compass. Well, it turns out that many government funded labs were paid and allowed to experiment on many black people for the possible purpose of population control.

Whatever the mindset, madness, mission, or methods, for some reason, God has not allowed the entire black population to be destroyed. While white Americans have certainly been able to decimate millions of our people, they have not succeeded at total genocide or apartheid.

What are we to say then other than this is business as usual, or the price paid for being born black, because we see all too often that anything can be done to or against black people with absolutely no prosecution of those involved. The Tuskegee Syphilis experiment is one clear indication that this type of testing has been going on quite some time, and it has only come to the surface because people began asking questions and finding evidence.

Overcoming Oppression in America

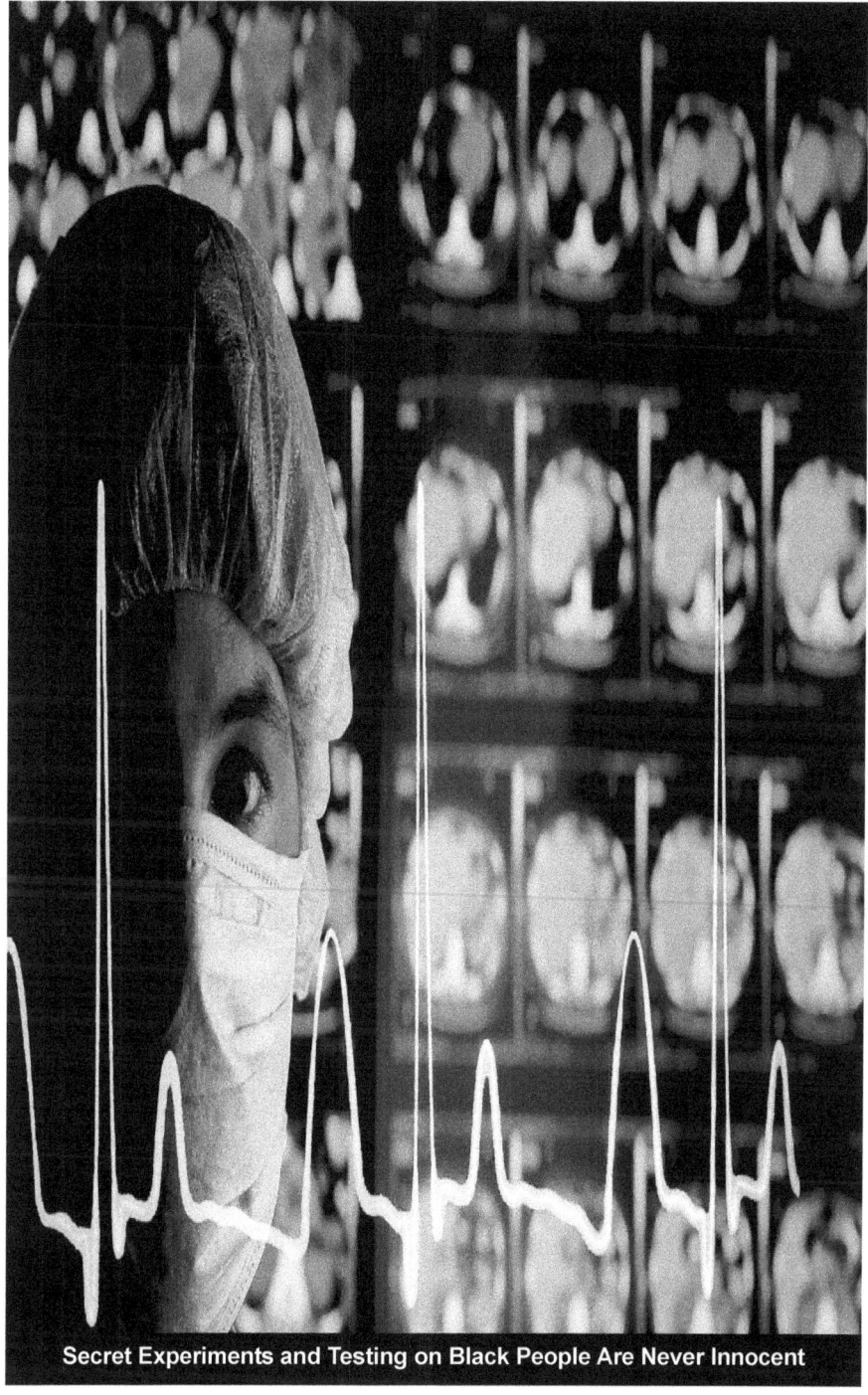

Secret Experiments and Testing on Black People Are Never Innocent

MONITOR AND SABOTAGE THEIR EVERY MOVEMENT

How do you fight an enemy you can't see? How do you fight an enemy who is intent upon doing everything they can, using every tool they can, to monitor your every movement, and in many cases sabotage your every attempt to make progress?

Black people have been experiencing the effects of such tactics our entire lives. Many of us, especially any of our leaders who are still living, are well aware that white Americans with hatred in their hearts have been using technology and other tools to keep tabs on our people for centuries.

Monitoring our movements includes but has not been limited to following us around in stores, tailing us when traveling to and from places we go, tapping our phone lines, bugging our email accounts, and placing Trojans inside our computers to monitor who we contact and connect with, and also to screen capture our keystrokes and clicks.

This practice was sanctioned and approved centuries ago and the actions are still quite prevalent in American society today.

I've experienced various levels of such abuse of power at different times in my life and it still occurs today.

It's not longer important to me the reasons why it happens to me or other people I know, because I'm keenly aware of what white Americans with hatred in their hearts will do to keep themselves feeling as if they have one-upped black people.

Miscarriages of justice occurring in the lives of black people happen on a daily basis somewhere in America. Whether it is in the courtroom, or on the street with police officers, in the marketplaces, corporate headquarters, warehouses and factories, and a host of other places where it can take place, it is indeed happening.

It is a form of harassment that has been a norm in the lives of black people.

People I know that such attacks have happened to learn to ignore it and the ignorant people behind it. It is an invasion of privacy often funded and approved by corrupt government officials.

There are so many cases and incidents of suspected spying on black Americans that because we know that once we speak out our entire family become targets for murder, many of us are no longer interested in the risk.

Being a whistle-blower rarely gets you anywhere in this country, even though there are laws in place that support the process. But when the people you are unleashing information on, are some of the very people who are gathering the data, you fight a losing battle to get anyone to listen to your story or even take you seriously.

Many people believe there is no one within the U.S. Government who isn't corrupt. I'm certain that from the thousands upon thousands of blogs I've read over the years and news articles I've seen, and other things I've seen swept under the rug, that everyone knows by now how corrupt and evil white Americans with hatred in their hearts can be.

Learning to ignore it is the best defense against it. I've personally decided that if they are willing to monitor, murder, and sabotage their own people, me as a black man ought to simply be thankful that my family and I are still alive and well.

I'm not angry behind it. And I won't give them any additional power over me by making me stoop to their level and retaliate as it would be easy to do. We don't repay evil with evil. We simply leave room for God's wrath to come upon them with the hot burning coals of hell fire that will eventually land upon their heads.

Monitoring and Sabotage are tactics used by white Americans for centuries, and many of those individuals work within American politics. It is no secret that they monitor everyone else in the world in the name of national security, but when they abuse that power and authority to monitor and sabotage its own non-threatening citizens 'just because' black people are perceived to be a threat is utterly ridiculous.

HOPE AND ANECDOTES

- **Demonizing** black people is common in America. We see it won't end.
- **Dangerous** people with hatred in their hearts are in powerful positions.
- **Dedicating** our lives to making life better for everyone is our focus.
- **Destruction** of black slaves is not the end for their descendants.
- **Death** of black leaders is not the end for their children and grand-kids.
- **Document** each and every incident to always keep a record of history.
- **Defeat** is simply an opportunity to come back even stronger next time.

What can be done to reverse the reality that tools and tactics to monitor and sabotage black people are commonplace?

Monitoring and sabotage most like began during the days of slavery when white Americans with hatred in their hearts started to realize that the Underground Railroad existed, and that there were *normal* white Americans willing to hide slaves who were trying to escape captivity.

The tools and tactics grew as technology developed enabling them to use computers and smart devices to watch the activity of black people from a distance.

One of the most common forms of such surveillance is having black people followed by engaging an entire group of people to put a dragnet around their homes.

Eventually all of the strategies used against individual black Americans comes to an end by exposing it or by someone within the ranks of the group who is doing the monitoring and helping to sabotage, defects and feels guilty enough to tell the truth.

Again, regardless of what white Americans with hatred in their hearts do to me or to my family, we're just grateful to God that we are still alive each day.

Overcoming Oppression in America

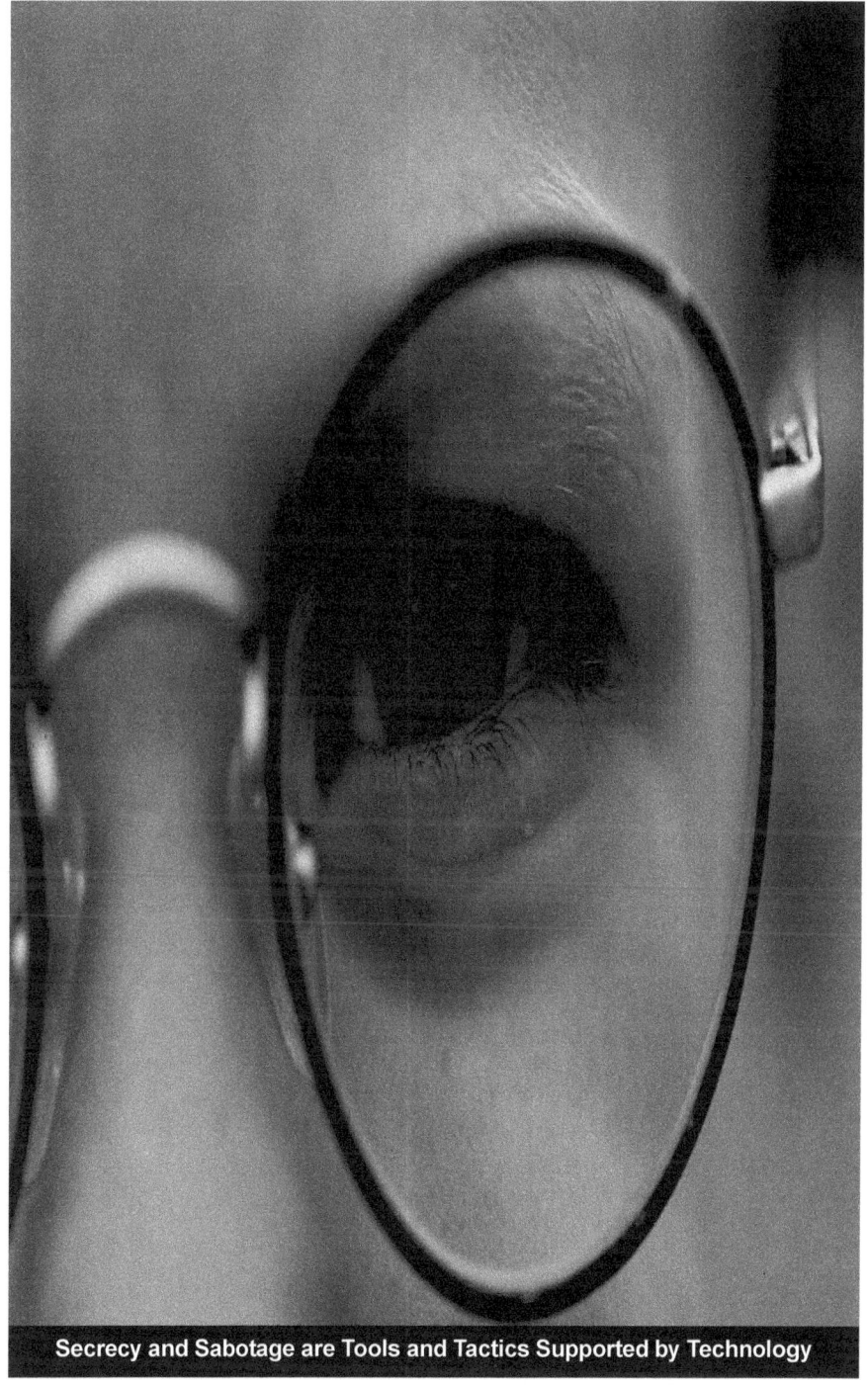

Secrecy and Sabotage are Tools and Tactics Supported by Technology

CALL ANYONE WHO TRIES TO HELP THEM N-LOVERS

There are many people who were and are not of color have stood arm-in-arm next to black Americans since the days of slavery. White Americans with hatred in their hearts have also had to face their own people, often from within their own families in the fight for civil and human rights.

We know from our horrific history that we've been called nearly every name in the book. But what you may not be aware of is that white Americans with hatred in their hearts also came up with some terms that they used to identify and harass and denigrate their own people if those people were taking a stand to help black folk in any way shape or form.

A few of those terms include:

N-LOVER

N-DIGGER

N-RIDER

OFAY

JUNGLE FEVER

SALT 'N PEPPER

BROWN BOMBER

If you look at the pictures or video from the civil rights movement you will see handfuls of non-black people who were willing to sacrifice their lives and safety to fight alongside black people for the cause. These numbers have increased dramatically over the past several decades. While some may think its a phenomenon, it actually is just the opposite. What we are witnessing is diversity, unity, and love in action, regardless of race, creed, color, culture, or sexual orientation. Human rights is human rights.

In fact, these days, if you look at some of the protests against white police officers killing unarmed and innocent black Americans, you're likely to see more white Americans protesting than you do black.

Black Americans have been showing up and participating in protests for decades. We know it typically doesn't change anything except to serve a purpose by exposing the continued wrongs being perpetrated by white Americans with hatred in their hearts.

Black Americans have been fighting this battle for centuries and we know it typically won't allow us to make any progress, but rather put us in a place of regress when we escalate such protests to the level of rioting and looting.

Rioting and looting are forms of internal frustration being expressed through external violence. While violence is never the answer, most people who riot and loot are often drawn into the action via a number of factors such as the *everybody's doing it so I will too* or *we deserve this given what little we have* or any of a variety of reasons.

However, when rioting and looting turn into violence against human beings, it makes those who riot and loot the same as those who committed the act against the black person or people, which started the protest to begin with.

Protests are very effective when done correctly, as long as they are peaceful, do not violate the law, and never puts any other people in harms way. Protests that tend to disrupt the common flow of traffic or disturb the peace in communities unrelated to the initial act against a black person or people are often seen as a waste of time and energy.

Rioting and looting against the resources in your own community after some white American with hatred in their hearts causes harm to or kills a black person, is narrow-minded. The individual who commits the act of violence in the form of a supremacy or hate crime, whether or not they are a police officer, likely lives in a residence in another community far away from the place that gets rioted or looted, is again, narrow-minded. Taking out your anger on someone other than the white person with hatred in their hearts who harmed a black person is ridiculous.

HOPE AND ANECDOTES

+ **Protesting** raises our voices, rioting and looting simply silences them.
+ **Peaceful** demonstrations were key to victory in the fight for civil rights.
+ **People** who hate because of people who hate are like people who hate.
+ **Presidents** should not be racist but rather compassionate to all citizens.
+ **Protect** yourself and family from those who want you dead or enslaved.
+ **Proclaim** freedom for those who never saw it in those of us left behind.
+ **Partner** with peacemakers standing against what is wrong in America.

---

*What can be done to reverse the reality
that name calling of anyone for any reason is always wrong?*

+

Protesting during times of slavery got black people killed.
Protesting in 2016 is still getting black people murdered.

+

Rioting and looting during civil rights robbed our own communities of resources.
Rioting and looting in 2016 is still robbing our communities of resources.

+

Name calling in slavery and civil rights was degrading and juvenile.
Name calling in 2016 is still degrading and juvenile.

+

During slavery and civil rights white people risked their lives helping black people.
In 2016 many white people are still risking their lives helping black folk.

At some point, life will have to either get better for black Americans, or it will become much worse. For the first time in our history, black men who were frustrated with the killing of black people by white police, took the law into their own hands and murdered police officers. This is completely wrong.

CHAPTER RECAP

+ Did the previous chapter teach you something?
+ Were you moved to want to want to help in some way?
+ Do you see any possible solutions to this issue?
+ Did these facts give you better understanding?
+ Does the hope suggested below offer apt solutions?
+ Share Comments: @WhiteHatredBlackHope

HATRED
Work Diligently to Crush Their Hopes and Dreams

HOPE
In the 2016 Olympics in Rio, a runner fell down during one of the races. In spite of the obstacle, he still won. You can do the same if you don't give up.

HATRED
Secretly Use Them to Test Drugs and Viruses

HOPE
As horrid as something like this is, it shouldn't shock you given all that we know. Don't let it stop you from pushing pass the pain into your purpose.

HATRED
Monitor and Sabotage Their Every Movement

HOPE
Some in the United States government treat its own citizens as if we are the enemy of this country. It has been happening since black people were stolen and enslaved. Keep praying and taking pride in all your work to change it.

HATRED
Call Anyone Who Tries to Help Them N-Lovers

HOPE
Regardless of what hateful people do to you or say about you, keep your head up and keep standing up against all that is wrong with America.

Section Two

BY FEAR

BY
FEAR

Impression
Seeing a black person who looks like you hanging from a tree with a noose around their neck can put fear in a person not strong enough to handle it. Witnessing a group of white people with hatred in their hearts standing outside your home with hoods on and carrying torches is also designed to instill fear.

Suggestion
The power of suggestion can wreak havoc on a person's mind if they aren't strong enough to handle it. Many of us know that fear is simply false evidence appearing real, but when you have heard, seen, and lived through decades of oppression, it is quite easy for those who are lording control over you to simply suggest what they can do to you to get you to comply.

Correction
Having been in prison I have experienced firsthand what happens to people who do not follow the rules and consider themselves higher than those in authority over them. The prison system is a place of 'correction' because it is designed to correct whatever behavior it was that landed you there in the first place and they can keep you there until they are ready to release you.

Insurrection
History has shown us and continues to prove to us that when black people protest against injustice in America, the laws continue to protect white Americans who commit the acts of injustice. Protesting doesn't prove anything, it simply gives those who are already intent upon hurting us a reason to escalate their intentions to a level that gets their message across.

CHAPTER TEN

USE MOLOTOV COCKTAILS TO DESTROY THEIR HOMES

Burning someones house down is arson and it is illegal. However, this was one of the methods used against black Americans in the past, and as recent as 2010 in the Midwest, a cross was burned on a black family's lawn. This madness was used to help instill fear in the people who lived in the places that were burned, even though they were shacks with no lights, running water, or modern amenities that most of us are now accustomed to.

Many times house were burned with people inside them, at night, while they were sleeping. If the black people living inside weren't killed by the fire or smoke inhalation, they were slaughtered by gunfire or burned when they tried to escape the fire inside their homes.

Like other supremacy and hate crimes that white Americans with hatred in their hearts have committed in this country, there never was any prosecution. People got away with murder for centuries and it was one of the primary ways to make black people fear their slavemasters and every white person.

A Molotov cocktail is typically made with a bottle of gasoline, or a bottle filled with alcohol, both of which burn much hotter and faster than if the home was to catch on fire from any other reason. Given that most of these residences were made of scrap wood, anytime they were set fire to, the fire decimated the entire structure and rarely left anything or anyone behind.

Actions such as arson was used as a way to keep slaves in line and complying with whatever their taskmasters said. Men, women, and children alike were subject to being burned at any time for any reason. As atrocious as that sounds, it is the reality of black life in America, and has been for many centuries.

Torches gave them light so the arsonists could see at night, and it not only led them to the places where slaves lived often in shacks on the plantation where they were forced to work, it would serve to aid them in burning their places of refuge down to force the slaves into compliance. Torches were especially used when whites searched for any slaves who tried to escape.

If you've never seen a body burned to a crisp by fire, it's not a sight for anyone who cannot stomach it. I'm not talking about the dummies and mannequins made up for television and movies, as it doesn't comes close to the real thing. My dad worked in a morgue and at a funeral home when I was younger, and I don't care to recall things I've seen and the stench I've smelled when he was at work embalming bodies in preparation for funerals.

My dad later died of respiratory failure and I believe it was directly related to all the chemicals he inhaled while working at some of the those places.

What slaves and black people in general have experienced over several centuries at the hands of white people with hatred in their hearts is nothing short of a travesty.

Each summer that I visited my grandmother, who lived in Osceola, Arkansas when my dad wasn't in the room, she would warn me and constantly remind me of what to look out for, and when to come running if I happened to wander too far away from the safety of her porch.

As a child raised in the sixties seeing images of black people hanging with nooses around their necks still affects me to this day. Although it no longer makes me fear white people, it angers me, but also makes me pity them.

The people they killed for sport were humble, simple people who were living in a foreign land where the only hope they had was to work and keep working until they could find a way to escape, or die trying.

I'm deeply saddened by the thoughts of what my ancestors and family members were forced to endure at the hands of hateful white people who cared about absolutely nothing but themselves, their profit, and their ideals.

+

They decimated entire black families for generations, and got away with it.

They killed generations of black families and always got away with it.

They enslaved millions of black people and got away with it.

HOPE AND ANECDOTES

- **Compliance** is one way to calm a crowd, but it doesn't remove the threat.
- **Cowards** choose to hide behind their methods of madness & mayhem.
- **Cancer** comes in many forms and two of them are bigotry and bias.
- **Crowds** can gather for either good or to do evil, which one is your choice.
- **Cocktails** are meant for drinking, not used to burn down buildings.
- **Creating** fear in some can be turned into cultivating freedom for all.
- **Coercion** was just one of the tactics used in slavery still used today.

What can be done to reverse the reality that black people can be burned out of our homes or burned in our homes?

Imagine that you are trying to lay down and go to sleep because you've labored so hard in the hot sun earlier in the day that you are now exhausted.

While you are trying to lay down and rest, you know that you cannot go to sleep because the moment you do, there is the likelihood that you will be awakened in alert to people outside your home with torches, or cross burning, in the middle of the night.

They could be there to take your wife and possibly your children to a place where they will rape them and send them back to you abused and bruised. If they aren't there on this night for sexual gratification, they are there to simply scare you for sport, or this might be the night they actually burn your house down, leaving you with nowhere to live except in the shack of another family or group of slaves who are lucky to still have a roof over their head, if they don't lynch you instead.

This is just a glimpse into the reality black people and our ancestors lived with all our lives. As black people, even today in 2016, this fear has also moved outside in that each time we leave our home knowing that an officer could pull us over and cause our nightmares to become all too real.

Overcoming Oppression in America

Weapon of Mindless Destruction

DRESS UP IN HOODS & LYNCH THEM TO ENHANCE FEAR

Private organizations have been around for centuries. However, some of these groups take their mission, vision, and objectives to another level by using their power and personal prejudices against black Americans.

It's 2016, and periodically in the media you'll read news reports of KKK rallies and other white supremacy events taking place all over the country. The only difference is that today, protestors are showing up at the rallies and expressing their disdain at the very thought that given all the atrocities that have taken place against black Americans, that anyone would still want to continue this blatantly racist and bigoted stand.

In recent days, fights have broken out at the events, with many of the members of the Klan being harmed by the protestors. While I don't know the details, what I've learned from glancing at the headlines in passing is that people are fed up with the actions particularly not only because of what they represent, but in countless incidents in our history, the group is directly responsible for killing an innumerable amount of people, both black and white alike.

Some of the disgust spills over into the fact that none of the hate or supremacy crimes have ever been prosecuted and people are tired, frustrated, and altogether fed up with racist white Americans being allowed to do anything to anyone they want to without recourse or retribution.

The fear of the past is no longer in most cases as people are willing to stand together and put their lives on the line to show solidarity and support for one another, and rally around black Americans in this issue.

Injustice is certainly still taking place though the fight against it has all but morphed into a national and even global effort to cut it off at the neck of the very hood still attempting to covering it.

Again, private organizations and supremacy and hate groups have been around for centuries. The exception is that people of all races and cultures who finally understand how wrong the proclivities of such racist group are, they are uniting with opposite but equally expressive passion and purpose against the hate.

Hatred has been the catalyst of harm against black Americans for centuries. While we still have yet to find an answer for the initial impetus, we know that hatred starts in the heart, and greed starts in the mind, and combining these two elements can create a mutated sense of sanity.

This mutated sense of sanity escalates into often uncontrollable and indecent acts against human beings, and because the people being affected are of a different color, class, or culture, they become the target.

The targeted group is faced with the mutated group's outward expression, and in this case, robes and hoods are the uniform; three letters represent the name; torches and burned crosses are the calling card; bigotry and bias are the values; and lynching and other forms of murder is the way to express those values.

mutated thoughts + mutated ideals = obscured vision.

Although the members of such hate and supremacy groups can function quite well in the general population we call society, their vision is obscured by hate and bigotry and bias, which makes them blind to any value the members of the targeted group possess.

Because members of the hate and supremacy groups believe that the targeted group has no value they are of the mindset that they need to be the ones to eliminate the target group, thereby *cleansing* the population of their color and contribution and any opportunity to 'taint' the supremacy group.

Such idealism is tainted at its core and the mission, vision, values and objectives are skewed by the very fact that you cannot cleanse an entire country, continent, or planet of any one group or another. If any group had the power to accomplish this, it would surely have been done given the massive amount of murder and mayhem inflicted on the target group over several centuries.

HOPE AND ANECDOTES

+ **Fire** can burn forever, just like the bigotry and bias lit long ago.
+ **Freedom** stands firmly in the face of and fights against fascism.
+ **Fresh** ideas come from forward think not backwards attitudes & antics.
+ **From** the beginning of the colonization of the U.S. hatred has harmed.
+ **Fallacies** cloud a sane person's ideals and turns them into illusions.
+ **Flames** create light to illuminate the darkness around it, ironic isn't it?
+ **Fractions** are simply part of the whole of a collective in a common factor.

What can be done to reverse the reality
that the Klan is still spreading hatred and killing black people today?

I've been a member of many groups, sat as a member on many boards of directors, and been the launcher and leader of many nonprofits, but I've never once hid my participation in anything.

If you're a member of something and you have to hide the fact that you are indeed signatory to that group, it would seriously make me wonder about the motives of the group regardless of whether or not our ideals align.

I've always wondered why members of the Klan hide the fact that they are racist, white supremacists, devoted to their cause.

The very fact that they escaped prosecution has made them above the law for so many centuries that it matters not that people know who they are.

My dad always taught me, take responsibility for your actions, stand up for what is right, be proud of who you are and where you come from, fight against any and everything that is morally and ethically wrong. These are just a few of the basics of living life in America as a member of this society, and as a citizen of this country, and I cannot in my right mind, find any reason whatsoever to hide that under a hood.

Overcoming Oppression in America

If You Were Proud Of Your Purpose You Wouldn't Have To Hide Under Hoods

BURN CROSSES ON THEIR LAWNS TO DENY THEIR GOD

The cross has been a spiritual symbol which represents Christians as followers of Christ for centuries. Where hate and supremacy groups got the idiotic idea to burn the cross as a symbol of their defiance and hatred is beyond my wildest attempts to find reasoning in it.

According to several sources such groups claim that the practice of burning crosses is supposed to be a symbol of their religious faith, but other sources say the ritual is simply an effort to intimidate anyone who does not agree with the groups beliefs.

At one point, in some of their documentation they consider themselves the true followers of Christ, which is contradictory because burning a cross symbolizes defiance of the symbol, not support of it.

Like flag burning is to most if not all Americans, cross burning is considered sacrilege to most if not all Christians.

I said in an earlier chapter that hate and supremacy groups have a mutated mindset, so its no surprise that they have skewed the meaning of their own ceremony.

The updated versions of such documentation now omits the word 'burning' and has been replaced with the word 'lighting'. So the ritual hasn't stopped, just the way it is referenced.

Cross burning or the aforementioned cross lighting has served as a symbol of hate from the beginning of the colonization of this country. One has to wonder who had the first thought to initiate such an act, and what it was that they referenced to make their thinking travel down this road.

Common sense typically does not exist in senseless acts. Cross burning in my opinion is no different than rioting and looting and setting fire to the stores, shops and resources in ones own community when protesting. To me, they are one in the same set of sadistic ideals that need to be banished.

However, our history as black Americans proves that punishment of cross burning has rarely been assessed, though jailing black people for protesting, rioting, looting, and arson during expressions of frustration has become the norm.

How can one group get away with their actions and the other does not? Simple. It has been the method of operation of the criminal justice system since its inception, and I believe that the reason for this is that many members of hate groups are also members of the justice system.

Thus, if they were to punish hate groups for their actions, in effect they would be punishing themselves.

> *The justice system rarely adjudicates injustice within the justice system. They simply find a way to justify the injustice as justifiable.*

God is not mocked and He is no respecter of persons. So, after the cross has been lit and burned, and the group has gone home for the night, He is and always will be, God.

Burning the cross has no effect on Him.

He created the wood the cross is likely built out of, and He created the fire with which the wood is burned. And, He created the people whose minds have been given over to a reprobate reality. He also created the fabric with which members of such hate groups create clothes to hide themselves. And, He created the shoes they wear on their feet to walk to, participate in, and walk away from, such events. He created the globe, the water, the continents, the land, water, air, and all the other elements around us. It is all His anyway.

Such hate groups that consider themselves burning the cross in defiance of God's choice to create black people, are simply showing Him how ignorant they are. Black is not the only race on the planet, and targeting black people shows even further how narrow-minded such thinking is, especially given that blacks are already considered as having the least amount of resources historically, across the globe. Why we are a target of such supremacy groups, again, is beyond my wildest attempts to find reasoning in it.

HOPE AND ANECDOTES

+ **Hours** mark the turn of the clock, and many wish to turn it backwards.
+ **Hurt** never heals as long as the scab covering it keeps being picked at.
+ **How** can we all move forward when one group won't move out the way.
+ **Hasten** to the triage that is a hospital and help for the spiritually sick.
+ **Horrific** images of hatred past and present hurt me, do they upset you?
+ **Honesty** is always the best policy even when its built on layers of lies.
+ **Hear** the men, women & children who sacrificed their lives for all of us.

---

*What can be done to reverse the reality
that the Klan is still defying God who is love by practicing hate?*

Imagine you went to work today, left your job, came home and pulled into your driveway or parked in front of your home. You exit the car and notice that there's a glow behind your house, and the smell of a burning fire is in the air.

You think nothing of it, because the neighbors are usually outside using their fire pit to roast marshmallows, but you don't see them.

You search for the right key to open your front door, turn it, go inside and before you can turn the lights on, you notice that same glow from outside is inside your house.

Now you start to wonder. It's quiet and there's no sound of a fire truck heading in your direction.

You decide to open the blinds covering the sliding glass of the back door.

You see that the glow of fire is in your back yard, in the form of a cross, and it is burning. There's no one out there, but it is clear that someone has been there.

Overcoming Oppression in America

It's Not What You See in This Image it's What It Says

KILL THEIR LEADERS TO MAKE THEM FEAR SPEAKING OUT

I remember exactly where I was the day the news of Dr. King being assassinated came across the television in a news report. I was five years old. I was standing in the dining room of our home on Throop Street.

There was such a scream that echoed throughout the neighborhood that it put fear in me. And then there was silence.

The looks on the faces of members of my family and everyone I saw for what seemed like the next several weeks, were disbelief and shock and hurt and sadness and pain. Tears flowed and eyes welled with water, but no one made a sound.

White Americans with hatred in their hearts were responsible for the death of Dr. King, regardless of who they say actually pulled the trigger. To them he was just another N*#%. To all of black America, he was the one willing to stand on the front line, shout from the rooftop, and take the message of freedom to all Americans from church to church, city to city, state to state.

Fast forward to 2016, and although the 48 years may seem to have put distance between that day and these, when black leaders get murdered for simply standing up against racism, hatred, bigotry and bias, one death affects us all.

We've lost so many leaders over the centuries, innumerable, and yet each one is remembered. We suffer in silence but continue to raise our voices to the reality of racism.

Hatred of black Americans by white Americans with hatred in their hearts is not dead, and the fact that many black leaders are, in 2016, proves it. You may not keep as close a watch on the news reports as others, but we see the headlines are no different from what they read back then. White Americans with hatred in their hearts are still riding the wave of racism in America, over the lives of black people, and we as black Americans know that the blood of our ancestors and even today's leaders, will never dry up.

I believe if Dr. King were alive today he would high five and hug Obama as a symbol and gesture of hope. However, if King were to dig a little deeper and read some of the headlines littered in cities all over America, even in many northern states, he would quickly realize the battleground against bigotry has spread from the streets of Montgomery to Main Street America.

He would soon recognize that the movements of today have grown from the sectors of the south to pockets of protests all over the world.

The work he started is still going, and we have not yet fully seen the fruit of his labor in the form of the unity and cohesiveness of black people and white people coming together to fight against oppression, because the fight is still underway.

48 years after his death in 1968 the fight for civil and human rights is still day by day. Some days are better than others but depending on who you ask they are all bad. Protests, rioting, looting, are still taking place, only because white Americans with hatred in their hearts only seem to care about race.

Bigotry is still headline news.
Bias is still the schools.

Black people are still being killed.
Caskets and graveyards are still being filled.

Blood is still staining the ground.
Racism is still hanging around.

The dream is still very much alive and well.
The vision behind it still a daily story to tell.

Black lives do not matter to those who are on a killing spree.
They only see the color of who we are not who we could be.

Systemic injustice and injustice with the system reign.
Moms, dads, brothers and sisters, all still in pain.

HOPE AND ANECDOTES

- **Malice** lives in the hearts of those who hate and hurt others for no reason.
- **Murder** is their method and madness and mayhem is their motivation.
- **Moving** north no longer makes us safe because hate has spread all over.
- **Maligned** from north to south, east to west, no place is immune from it.
- **Meaningless** murders take place everywhere, even in our children still.
- **Mourning** & grieving will never satisfy the never-ending pain we feel.
- **Mending** the scars with strength is still our band-aid after the burial.

What can be done to reverse the reality that assassinating black leaders is still taking place in 2016?

Speaking out against oppression can get you killed. Speaking out against police brutality and the murder of unarmed and innocent black people can get you killed. Being born black can get you killed. Getting pulled over by the police for just a traffic stop can get you killed.

This is just a handful of the many scenarios that have been taking place in the black community for centuries. Murder is the method and madness and mayhem is the motivation of white Americans with hatred in their hearts toward black Americans.

The depth of this reality has always made me want to live in another country but the same hatred that white Americans have lathered upon black people, they have also spread to numerous other nations as well.

Black Americans languish over the fact that we still in 2016 are not truly free from hate. We have to watch ourselves everywhere we go, in all that we do, and with what we say.

We can be killed anywhere by anyone, and all too often it is at the hand of those in authority who are paid to serve and protect everyone.

Overcoming Oppression in America

CHAPTER RECAP

+ Did the previous chapter teach you something?
+ Were you moved to want to want to help in some way?
+ Do you see any possible solutions to this issue?
+ Did these facts give you better understanding?
+ Does the hope suggested below offer apt solutions?
+ Share Comments: @WhiteHatredBlackHope

HATRED
Use Torches and Molotov Cocktails to Destroy Their Homes

HOPE
Prosecuting people who commit such heinous acts with real justive via hate and supremacy crime laws may deter others from doing it in the future.

HATRED
Dress Up in Hoods and Lynch Them to Enhance Fear

HOPE
The robes and hoods are still around, but they are being met with severe opposition at their events, rallies, and recruiting sessions. This is progress.

HATRED
Burn Crosses on Their Lawns to Deny Their God

HOPE
We have always hoped that the United States Government would step in and make laws to have this classified this as symbolic sacrilege and put away the people who do it at prison camps with the other political prisoners.

HATRED
Kill Their Leaders to Make Them Fear Speaking Out

HOPE
In 2016 black people who step up to be leaders are still being killed. While they may die as martyrs for the cause, there still is no cause for their death.

Section Three

BY FAITH

BY FAITH

Overcome
In order to win the battle against bigotry and bias against black Americans everyone in America with a love for people regardless of who they are, what they look like, where they live, what color or culture they are from, we all have to work to overcome evil with good, and indeed we shall overcome.

Outlast
America was born, built, and broken on the backs of slaves. In order to build it up again, everyone who wants a better country has to work together to stand up against hate and white supremacy so we can outlast this long-standing attack on our own citizens with longevity and longsuffering.

Outshine
Actions speak much louder than words. We have to love our neighbor in our actions, help through our actions. Live right by our actions. Make life better for everyone by our actions. For it is the only way to outshine those who are selfish and greedy and only want America for themselves.

Overwhelm
Love needs to be the foundation of everything we do in America. With this in mind, it becomes easier to love our enemies, love those who hate us, love our neighbor as we love ourselves, and overwhelm someone with love simply because it is the right thing to do when they attack us with hate.

Outperform
Standing in the gap for others means that when they can't do it, we step up and help them push through it. We have to make America the opposite of a self-centered society where you rarely see fellow man helping fellow man. We have to outperform those at the top with their gauge of greed by being ten times more humble, so humility affects everyone it touches, even them.

CHAPTER ELEVEN

FAITH HOPE AND CHARITY

How do you get your enemy to pay attention to you long enough to listen to your viewpoint? How do you show your value to someone who is dead set upon destroying you, any and everything you do, and making sure that you never participate in any part of society in any way ever?

Answer: You don't.

If you focus your life on what your enemy wants to do to you or what they are already doing to you or what power they may have over you or what potential problems they can cause for you, you will spend your entire life doing absolutely nothing.

Your entire energy will be focused on reaction rather than action. If you spend your time walking forward, you are being productive. If you focus on reaction, you will always be in a mode of regress rather than making progress.

In 1st Corinthians 13:13 the Bible says *And now abideth faith, hope, charity, these three; but the greatest of these is charity.*

Faith is the substance of things hoped for, the evidence of things not seen.

For we are saved by **Hope**: but hope that is seen is not hope: for what a man seeth, why doth he yet hope for?

Charity is taught in many ways in the Bible. My favorite is:
- + For I was an hungred, and ye gave me meat:
- + I was thirsty and ye gave me drink:
- + I was a stranger and ye took me in:
- + Naked, and ye clothed me:
- + I was sick, and ye visited me:
- + I was in prison, and ye came unto me.

I've written several books on each of these subjects, but for the purpose of this book *White Hatred Black Hope* I will focus my thoughts here.

Faith in this scripture is identified in Hebrews 11:1.
Hope in this text is explained in Romans 8:24.
Charity in this lesson is detailed in Matthew 25: 35-36.

Each of these scriptures tell of the incredible plight of black Americans.

Faith is why we believe God will deliver us from the destroyer.

Hope is how we remain confident in our conditions.

Charity is what we do to help others and in it we are helped.

I've always been convinced from the time in Junior High when I started recognizing that my abilities both academically and athletically, were far above anyone around me, that black people were never meant to live our lives as the footstool for white people, the punching post for white people, the bean bag for white people, the guinea pigs for white people, the funeral fillers for white people.

Black people are gifted, talented, skilled, with so many abilities, creativity, intelligence, rhythm, and innovation, that it became easy to see why white people have always wanted to keep what is naturally inside of us suppressed.

Everything we do we excel at. We far exceed expectation on just about any project or platform. It is partly the reason why white people with hatred in their hearts have always worked diligently to keep us down, because they fear what we become when we are able to rise up.

One of my favorite poems is Maya Angelou's *Still I Rise*.
One of my favorite songs is Audra Day's *Rise Up*.
Each of these embody the struggle and the strength black people possess, to enable us to endure all we've ever gone through and still live with today in 2016. The passion and prose in the words to both this poem and song have given me strength on many a dreary day, and sleepless night, when I've stayed awake from frustration and anger, crying tears from my belly behind yet another report of violence against yet another black person, especially when they lose their life because of the actions of yet another white person.

SUGGESTED SOLUTIONS

+ **Ignoring** evidence & moving forward in spite of is difficult but necessary.
+ **Initiate** new paths to progress, race forward and don't run backwards.
+ **Instill** faith, hope and charity in your children and teach them to pray.
+ **Inject** truth into all you do, and let lies & legends fall where they may.
+ **Increase** and enlarge your territory through Biblical and social circles.
+ **Insist** upon doing the right thing and don't settle for anything less.
+ **Inhale** the power, take in the promise, and learn to exhale the problems.

What can be done to embrace the evidence
and still move forward in spite of the opposition and oppression?

Living as black Americans in this society, we have to learn how to get through and get past all that is continuously done to us to set us back, so that we can continue to move forward.

We have to learn to focus on God's promises and let Him worry about and deal with the problems.

When we focus on our faith...
When we help each other have hope...
When we give ourselves over to charity...

...we take away the power that white people with hatred in their hearts think they have over us. We rise up to a much higher level than the bottom-feeder thinking that always has them focused on us.

When we learn to act instead of react, we rise above our past, our present, and begin to press toward our future.

Those who seek to destroy us, are simply being used to push and propel us into our destiny.

Overcoming Oppression in America

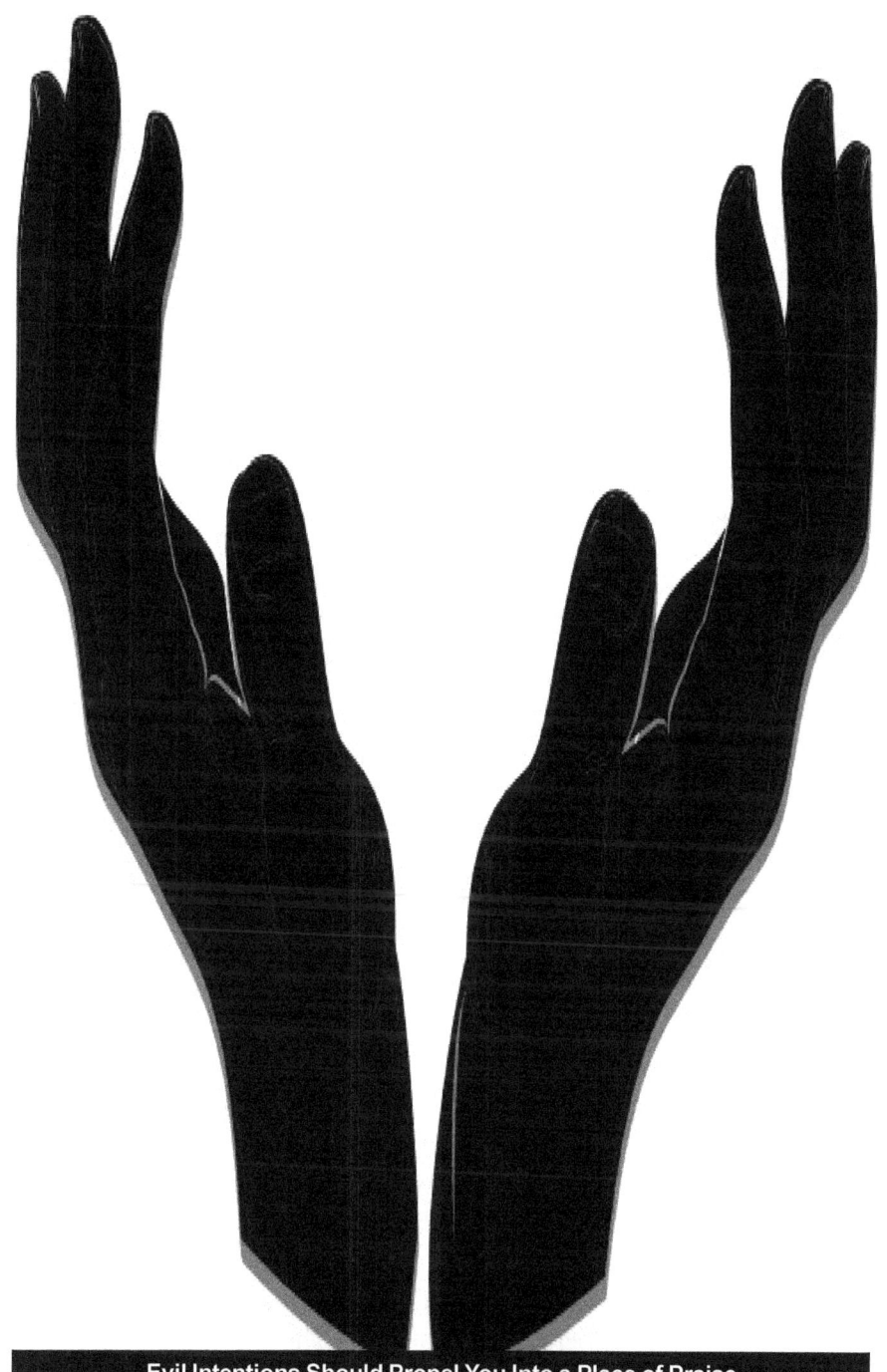

LOVE YOUR ENEMY

Imagine being told from the time you were born into the world that you were hated simply because of the color you were born with, and soon after that comes your first days of school and they show you that you are going to face an enemy that is going to work diligently to steal, kill, and destroy everything you do, including but not limited to murdering some or all of your family members, again, all because of the color of your skin.

Then on another day, when you begin to question why, someone else comes along and tells you that in spite of all that you've gone through, and what you will face, you must love your enemy.

They tell you that in this book called the Bible, which you are to learn from, get wise about, and let it be the barometer for your life, a scripture known as Matthew 5:44 says:

> *Love Your Enemies*
> *Bless Them That Curse You*
> *Do Good To Them That Hate You*
> *and*
> *Pray For Them Which Despitefully Use You*
> *And Persecute You*

What would your response be? Would you believe them? Would you do all you can to fight against what they say you should do to help you get through all you're destined to go through?

And let's say that one day you finally get sick and tired of being fed up and frustrated at the blatant disregard for you as a person, an individual, with hope and dreams. Knowing that there is an entire culture of people who hate you simply because of the color of your skin.

So you decide that because nothing else has worked, and you are constantly reminded of what that person told you about the tool to use to give you power over your enemies, that you decide to give in and give it a try.

They told you it was not going to be easy to love your enemies, but knowing nothing else has worked, you make the decision to learn how.

LOVE YOUR ENEMIES
They hate you because of the color of your skin. It's difficult but documented. There is deliverance in death. They are dangerous so you be determined.

BLESS THEM THAT CURSE YOU
You will be spit on, pushed around, and called more names than I can mention. Learn to ignore it. Bless them instead. Don't repay evil with evil.

DO GOOD TO THEM THAT HATE YOU
They hurt you, you heal them. They hate you, you love them. They push you, you pray for them. It's not easy but it is quite necessary.

PRAY FOR THEM WHICH DESPITEFULLY USE YOU
Prayer is a powerful tool to use against anything you're going through. God hears & answers prayer as long as you're praying in faith for what you ask.

AND PERSECUTE YOU
Remember to press, eyes on the prize, the promise, the process, the preparation comes through persecution now, is for a celebration in the end.

+++

You may say to yourself, *Lord you are asking a whole lot*. And knowing Him, the response you'll likely receive will be to the effect that *They hate you because of me* or *Leave room for my wrath* or *No weapon formed against thee shall prosper; and every tongue that shall rise against thee in judgment thou shalt condemn. This is the heritage of the servants of the Lord, and their righteousness is of me, saith the Lord.*

So, now that you know, what will you do with the knowledge you've received?

Will you receive the word the way it was written?
Will you continue to push through the pain?
Will you embrace eternity instead of Earth?
Will you learn to love them?
Will you forgive them?

SUGGESTED SOLUTIONS

- **Torches** are meant to burn, but we can use them to light our way.
- **Testimony** can help others get through, what you have gone through.
- **Talk** to each other so that you can listen and learn from one another.
- **Task** yourself each day to push higher, work harder, and pray stronger.
- **Time** heals all wounds, but only if you bring the hurt to the surface.
- **Turning** the other cheek shows they didn't hurt you with the first blow.
- **Terminate** any thoughts to retaliate but rather restore what they destroy.

What can be done to embrace the evidence and educate your enemies while you endure to eternity?

The actions of white Americans with hatred in their hearts toward black people are deplorable. This is a fact that we have known for centuries.

+ I know its a problem because it continues to happen.
+ I know its difficult to love them knowing they hate us.
+ I know its not easy to smile while crying inside.

We have to continue to endure for those who come after us. Those who came before us toughed it out so that we could be here today, reading words such as these, and living the life we're living. We are not completely free, but we're better off than they were. Each generation will get better, but this one is not it. Maybe the next generation, but I humbly, firmly, and honestly believe that it will take another three to four generations, meaning another three to four hundred years for black people to be free of bigotry and bias from hateful white people. I'll say it again, this is not the generation that we will be completely free. We're not going to wake up one morning and the world will be different. It doesn't work that way. It's a very slow process. It took generations to get here, and it will take more generations to get there. Be honest and real with yourself, and help others learn this as well and we all will be OK in the end.

Overcoming Oppression in America

BLACK BOY: "I'm Taught To Love You Even Though You're Told To Hate Me"

LIFT UP YOUR EYES TO THE HILLS

Can you be confident in your conditions? Can you still remain resolute and resilient in spite of what people who hate you do to you? Can you continue loving them even though they hate you? White Americans with hatred in their hearts toward black Americans may never change, are you OK with that?

I mentioned earlier that if you focus all your energy on them you'll never make progress for you. You'll be too distracted by the centuries of hateful things they've been taught to do to you. You'll be too unbalanced from the blows they throw to be grounded enough to take them.

In the book of Psalm chapter 121 verse 1, the Bible teaches us to say:

> *I will lift up mine eyes unto the hills, from whence cometh my help.*
> *My help cometh from the Lord, which made heaven and earth.*

Anytime I've taught Bible study class, especially to black American adults, I've placed emphasis on helping them to keep their faith and focus on God. I do my best to teach them, or help them to learn how to not focus on anything that white Americans with hatred in their hearts can do, or will do to them.

Here are some of the points I've made to students over the years:

Placing your faith in God forces your focus to follow.

Lifting your eyes up to the hills helps you forget those in the valley.

No one can do any harm to your soul, even if they torture your body.

Reading this scripture prompts us to look higher than our enemy for our help.

Your eyes are typically attracted to what you tell them to look at. That focus starts inside, in your heart, speaks to your mind, then manifests itself in action out through your eyes. Change your focus & what your eyes look at.

There are more than enough elements around the hills to keep your focus away from anything other than God.

Some of those elements include:

- Sun
- Moon
- Stars
- Clouds
- Mountains
- Waterfalls
- Forests
- Rocks
- Streams
- Rivers
- Sand
- Eagles

> 12 Things God Created To Help Us Relax, Relate, and Remain Resolute in Any Condition.

These are just twelve things that you can focus on that will keep you from being burdened by bias and bigotry. These are peaceful things that God created to help us to keep our faith and focus on Him, and not on anyone or anything others attempt to do to you.

I do my absolute best to get outside as much as I possibly can even when I'm writing lots of books because it helps me to relax, relate, and reverence God for who He is and all that He does in my life in spite of those who hate me.

SUGGESTED SOLUTIONS

+ **Sunshine** even on an overcast day, still provides light for you to look at.
+ **Staying** relaxed, resilient, resolute, reticent, helps you reverence God.
+ **Soothing** yourself by going camping is how I kept my family focused.
+ **Strength** can come from recharging your battery by getting outdoors.
+ **Spending** time outside eases your mind and helps you focus inside.
+ **Senses** respond to what you show them, may it always be peaceful.
+ **Specialize** in keeping soft sounds and music, around you at all times.

---

*What can be done to embrace the elements
and enjoy your surroundings until the Lord returns?*

At one point in my life, for a full year, I stopped watching television news. I forced myself away from it. It helped me more than I can explain to you.

Much of what we are affected by comes from what we see and hear and most of that comes from images and sounds that we can turn off.

Relaxation can help you stay focused on God rather than anything else that is going on in this world. The fact that you cannot fix the world, no matter how hard you try, should at least let you know that you don't have to be the one to worry about it either.

Racism, hatred, bias, bigotry, and everything that goes along with it do not have to be your focus at any time. You can live the vast majority of your life disconnected from any demonic or devilish or destructive activity if you just keep your faith in God, your focus off the world, and your feet moving away from anything that can be a distraction.

Get outside, away from all the noise, and embrace nature in a way that you may never have before. Let it be the renewing of your mind and the peace that passes all understanding because it can truly guard your heart & mind.

There Are Places All Over the Planet To Go and Enjoy God.

FRET NOT BECAUSE OF EVIL DOERS

Mowing the lawn is a peaceful time for me. I see people passing by, including at times some of my enemies, but I stay focused because it helps me to know and understand that grass is used as a metaphor in one of the most impactful passages of scripture in my life.

Psalm chapter 37 has been connected to me in some way since I was 34 years old. If you've read or heard any of my testimony by reading any of the dozens of books I've written or the dozen of videos or Podcasts I've produced, you would hear me make this statement from the following verse:

> *Fret not thyself because of evildoers,*
> *neither be thou envious against the workers of iniquity.*
>
> *For they shall soon be cut down like* **grass***,*
> *and wither as the green herb.*
>
> *Trust in the Lord and do good;*
> *so shalt thou dwell in the land,*
> *and verily thou shalt be fed.*
>
> *Delight thyself also in the Lord:*
> *and He shall give thee the desires of thine heart.*
>
> *Commit thy way unto the Lord;*
> *trust also in Him;*
> *and He shall bring it to pass.*

Before I continue with the rest of this vitally important chapter of scripture, I want you to understand the context as you are reading through it.

God knows His people suffered in the past, and He sees the suffering of His saints today. He never said this life would be easy, and His reminders that He will never leave us nor forsake us are all around us. We have to endure to the end in order to see that which He has laid up for us in eternity.

*And he shall bring forth thy righteousness as the light,
and thy judgment as the noonday.
Rest in the LORD, and wait patiently for him:
fret not thyself because of him who prospereth in his way,
because of the man who bringeth wicked devices to pass.
Cease from anger, and forsake wrath: fret not thyself in any wise to do evil.
For evildoers shall be cut off: but those that wait upon the LORD,
they shall inherit the earth.
For yet a little while, and the wicked shall not be:
yea, thou shalt diligently consider his place, and it shall not be.
But the meek shall inherit the earth;
and shall delight themselves in the abundance of peace.
The wicked plotteth against the just, and gnasheth upon him with his teeth.
The Lord shall laugh at him: for he seeth that his day is coming.
The wicked have drawn out the sword, and have bent their bow,
to cast down the poor and needy, and to slay such as be of upright conversation.
Their sword shall enter into their own heart, and their bows shall be broken.
A little that a righteous man hath is better than the riches of many wicked.
For the arms of the wicked shall be broken: but the LORD upholdeth the righteous.
The LORD knoweth the days of the upright: and their inheritance shall be for ever.
They shall not be ashamed in the evil time:
and in the days of famine they shall be satisfied.
But the wicked shall perish, and the enemies of the LORD shall be as the fat of
lambs: they shall consume; into smoke shall they consume away.
The wicked borroweth, and payeth not again:
but the righteous sheweth mercy, and giveth.
For such as be blessed of him shall inherit the earth;
and they that be cursed of him shall be cut off.
The steps of a good man are ordered by the LORD: and he delighteth in his way.
Though he fall, he shall not be utterly cast down:
for the LORD upholdeth him with his hand.
I have been young, and now am old;
yet have I not seen the righteous forsaken, nor his seed begging bread.
He is ever merciful, and lendeth; and his seed is blessed.
Depart from evil, and do good; and dwell for evermore.
For the LORD loveth judgment, and forsaketh not his saints;
they are preserved for ever: but the seed of the wicked shall be cut off.*

SUGGESTED SOLUTIONS

+ **Effective** & effectual are two words taught about prayer in James 5:16.
+ **Energizing** through rest and relaxation keeps you peaceful & powerful.
+ **Educate** others on how to stop focusing and fretting over evil people.
+ **Emerge** victorious and you will spend little time worried about others.
+ **Eat** from scripture and it will strengthen your spirit inside and out.
+ **East** is just one point on a compass, there are three more to explore.
+ **Everything** around you is not meant for you to see or hear. Turn it off.

---

*What can be done to embrace the effortlessness
and remove yourself far away from the evil and the evildoers?*

---

*The righteous shall inherit the land, and dwell therein for ever.
The mouth of the righteous speaketh wisdom, and his tongue talketh of judgment.
The law of his God is in his heart; none of his steps shall slide.
The wicked watcheth the righteous, and seeketh to slay him.
The LORD will not leave him in his hand, nor condemn him when he is judged.
Wait on the LORD, and keep his way, and he shall exalt thee to inherit the land:
when the wicked are cut off, thou shalt see it.
I have seen the wicked in great power, and spreading himself like a green bay tree.
Yet he passed away, and, lo, he was not: yea, I sought him, but he could not be found.
Mark the perfect man, and behold the upright: for the end of that man is peace.
But the transgressors shall be destroyed together:
the end of the wicked shall be cut off.
But the salvation of the righteous is of the LORD:
he is their strength in the time of trouble.
And the LORD shall help them, and deliver them:
he shall deliver them from the wicked, and save them, because they trust in him.*

+ + +

We are the righteousness of God. If you can believe it you can receive it.
The Lord is on my side; I will not fear: what can man do unto me?
Psalm 118:6

Overcoming Oppression in America

Get Out There and Gravitate Toward God

CHAPTER RECAP

+ Did the previous chapter teach you something?
+ Were you moved to want to want to help in some way?
+ Do you see any possible solutions to this issue?
+ Did these facts give you better understanding?
+ Does the hope suggested below offer apt solutions?
+ Share Comments: @WhiteHatredBlackHope

SCRIPTURE
Faith Hope and Charity

HOPE
Give of yourself unto others. It can help keep you grounded and focused on someone and something other than all that is wrong in the world.

SCRIPTURE
Love Your Enemy

HOPE
This may be the most difficult thing for you to do in your life but it is necessary to help you to never become like those who hate you.

SCRIPTURE
I Will Lift Mine Eyes Unto The Hills

HOPE
Get outside and enjoy all that God has created for us to see. Travel east, go west, explore the north, see the south. It can help you to rest and relax and recharge so you will be ready to face anything that comes your way.

SCRIPTURE
Fret Not Thyself Because of Evildoers

HOPE
One of the most important passages of scriptures that has impacted my life for many years. I pray that you embrace it so it brings peace to you.

CHAPTER TWELVE

EPILOGUE

SUMMARY

In the 1970's Author Alex Haley did an incredible job of depicting the conditions that black people are subjected to. His book was adapted into an amazing film, and made it to the TV screens of every American household.

He also touched on the fate of those of non-black descent who attempted to step in and try to help black people in any way.

40 years later, the movie *The Help* did an equally awesome job at showing the state that black servants were in 'inside the house' when they could make it from the heat of the field outside to the hearth of a fireplace inside.

Not prosecuting closet racist individuals and groups set the precedent in the past, is continuing to perpetrate and condone their behavior in the present, and gives many of them the license, gun and badge to kill many more black people in the future. Yes, we are going to lose many more.

The battle for human and civil rights is now targeting both closet racism as well as systemic injustice and the battle ground now includes people of all races, colors, and creeds who understand one thing:

> *A cycle without an end is set to repeat itself.*
> *Unless we put an end to this it will continue.*

Think of it this way, any system that is turned on cannot turn itself off. It takes some other action to push the power button so it loses the connection to the power conduit and shuts down.

Hateful white people are the reason behind the plight and condition of black Americans living in poverty today. They caused the condition. They are the underlying reason for the result. Many have no remorse about their actions, and they seem not to have it in them to take responsibility. If I could pull the switch and send those who deserve it to Hell, I probably would. Yet, I have a heart of forgiveness. I know this battle vs bias & bigotry is not mine.

45 years after the movie *Roots*, the movie *Selma* also helped to open the eyes and minds of those who are still in denial about the inhumane treatment of black people over the past five hundred years.

I look back at the early parts of the book of Genesis and now know what God must have felt when He made the decision to destroy the people that lived back then by flooding the Earth. The same sin and selfishness still exists today, but it has gotten a thousand times worse.

We are supposed to love God and eschew evil. It's difficult not to be angry behind all this chaos when we serve the only One who has the power to do anything about it.

We pray for peace but it never comes. We pray for change and put our lives on the front lines in the form of protest to make a noise, yet change still never comes.

Our only hope, and the primary reason I wrote this book, is to continue to forgive, and to put my faith and focus and trust in God that the end of all mankind will come soon and that life in eternity is near.

May God continue to bless you and yours always and may He give you the strength to endure.

-OO-

POEM

If someone filled with hate ever takes my life
I pray the church would step in and help my wife.

After I'm gone don't protest about my rights
Just turn more of those who hate into candles and lights.

Ignite the fire within to burn down walls of hate
Show them how love conquers all and why it's not too late.

Use the energy to educate them about who we are
Teach them *why* the light within us comes from afar.

Train them on how to use non-violence in this battle
Remind them that we are people not to be treated like cattle.

This is a war that black people could never win.
It is imperative that we simply endure to the end.

No movement or methods will have any lasting impact.
No laws or statutes or any government measure in fact.

Can undo or prevent the chains on my feet and lashes on my back.
We have to look at them for who they are and why they attack.

Change has to take place deep within their hearts.
Loving your enemy is where it starts.

We could talk about and stress over this until the end.
But this is a war that black people can never ever win.

RESOURCES

VIDEOS

NOTE: The page on the author's website that contains the 'Internal Link' also includes the 'External Links' for these videos as well.

Charlie Rose
Aired May 2016 - Video #1
Interview with Michael Eric Dyson
INTERNAL LINK: PastorKeith.org/whitehatredblackhope

Blackish Episode Clip
Aired February 2016 - Video #2
The cast tackles teaching their kids the truth about America.
INTERNAL LINK: PastorKeith.org/whitehatredblackhope

All The Difference
Aired September 2016 - Video #3
Documentary about two black teens pursuing collegiate dreams
INTERNAL LINK: PastorKeith.org/whitehatredblackhope

Tavis Smiley
Aired January 2016 Part 1 - Video #4
Interview with the only two black Senators in America
INTERNAL LINK: PastorKeith.org/whitehatredblackhope

Tavis Smiley
Aired January 2016 Part 2 - Video #5
Interview with the only two black Senators in America
INTERNAL LINK: PastorKeith.org/whitehatredblackhope

Charlie Rose
Aired September 2016 - Video #6
Interview with the only two black Senators in America
INTERNAL LINK: PastorKeith.org/whitehatredblackhope

VIDEOS

NOTE: The page on the author's website that contains the 'Internal Link' also includes the 'External Links' for these videos as well.

CBS Sunday Morning
Aired September 2016 - Video #7
Featuring the New African American Museum in D.C.
INTERNAL LINK: PastorKeith.org/whitehatredblackhope

CBS News
Aired September 2016 - Video #8
Interview with African Museum Curator and Assistant Director
INTERNAL LINK: PastorKeith.org/whitehatredblackhope

CBS This Morning
Aired September 2016 - Video #9
Interview with U.S. Attorney General Loretta Lynch
INTERNAL LINK: PastorKeith.org/whitehatredblackhope

Tavis Smiley
Aired June 2016 - Video #10
Interview with D.L. Hugely
INTERNAL LINK: PastorKeith.org/whitehatredblackhope

The View
Aired June 2016 - Video #11
Interview with D.L. Hugely
INTERNAL LINK: PastorKeith.org/whitehatredblackhope

Who Is Black in America
Aired on CNN 2013 - Video #12
Soledad O'Brien interviews several people of color about their roots.
INTERNAL LINK: PastorKeith.org/whitehatredblackhope

VIDEOS

NOTE: The page on the author's website that contains the 'Internal Link' also includes the 'External Links' for these videos as well.

Many Rivers to Cross
Aired on PBS 2013 Part 1 - Video #12
Henry Louis Gates Jr. Multiple interviews about African American roots.
INTERNAL LINK: PastorKeith.org/whitehatredblackhope

Many Rivers to Cross
Aired on PBS 2013 Part 2 - Video #13
Henry Louis Gates Jr. Multiple interviews about African American roots.
INTERNAL LINK: PastorKeith.org/whitehatredblackhope

Many Rivers to Cross
Aired on PBS 2013 Part 3 - Video #14
Henry Louis Gates Jr. Multiple interviews about African American roots.
INTERNAL LINK: PastorKeith.org/whitehatredblackhope

Many Rivers to Cross
Aired on PBS 2013 Part 4 - Video #15
Henry Louis Gates Jr. Multiple interviews about African American roots.
INTERNAL LINK: PastorKeith.org/whitehatredblackhope

Many Rivers to Cross
Aired on PBS 2013 Part 5 - Video #16
Henry Louis Gates Jr. Multiple interviews about African American roots.
INTERNAL LINK: PastorKeith.org/whitehatredblackhope

Many Rivers to Cross
Aired on PBS 2013 Part 6 - Video #17
Henry Louis Gates Jr. Multiple interviews about African American roots.
INTERNAL LINK: PastorKeith.org/whitehatredblackhope

VIDEOS

NOTE: The page on the author's website that contains the 'Internal Link' also includes the 'External Links' for these videos as well.

African American Lives
Aired on PBS 2013 Part 1 - Video #18
Henry Louis Gates Jr. Multiple interviews about African American roots.
INTERNAL LINK: PastorKeith.org/whitehatredblackhope

African American Lives
Aired on PBS 2013 Part 2 - Video #19
Henry Louis Gates Jr. Multiple interviews about African American roots.
INTERNAL LINK: PastorKeith.org/whitehatredblackhope

African American Lives
Aired on PBS 2013 Part 3 - Video #20
Henry Louis Gates Jr. Multiple interviews about African American roots.
INTERNAL LINK: PastorKeith.org/whitehatredblackhope

African American Lives
Aired on PBS 2013 Part 4 - Video #21
Henry Louis Gates Jr. Multiple interviews about African American roots.
INTERNAL LINK: PastorKeith.org/whitehatredblackhope

Tavis Smiley
Being interviewed about black life and politics in America.
Aired 2016 - Video #22
INTERNAL LINK: PastorKeith.org/whitehatredblackhope

Tavis Smiley
Being interviewed about his book by Trevor Noah
Aired January 2016 - Video #23
INTERNAL LINK: PastorKeith.org/whitehatredblackhope

VIDEOS

NOTE: The page on the author's website that contains the 'Internal Link' also includes the 'External Links' for these videos as well.

Bishop TD Jakes
Grace to Be Grounded: Finances
Aired January 2016 - Video #24
INTERNAL LINK: PastorKeith.org/whitehatredblackhope

Mimi Gerges
Interview with Tavis Smiley on race in America
Aired January 2016 - Video #25
INTERNAL LINK: PastorKeith.org/whitehatredblackhope

Tavis Smiley
Interview with Author and Lawyer Connie Rice on policing and politics
Aired April 2016 - Video #26
INTERNAL LINK: PastorKeith.org/whitehatredblackhope

Tavis Smiley
Interview with Adam Nagourney on political climate in black America
Aired July 2016 - Video #27
INTERNAL LINK: PastorKeith.org/whitehatredblackhope

Actor Jesse Williams
Award Acceptance Speech on the climate of black America
Aired July 2016 - Video #28
INTERNAL LINK: PastorKeith.org/whitehatredblackhope

VIDEOS

NOTE: The page on the author's website that contains the 'Internal Link' also includes the 'External Links' for these videos as well.

The Past is Alive Within Us
Documentary on the U.S. Dakota Conflict
Produced March 2014 - Video #29
INTERNAL LINK: PastorKeith.org/whitehatredblackhope

Author Keith Hammond
Preview of the book White Hatred Black Hope
Produced October 2014 - Video #30
INTERNAL LINK: PastorKeith.org/whitehatredblackhope

VIDEO DISCLAIMER:
I do not own any of the videos, links, references, and or other descriptions or otherwise contained on the previous pages and they are herein included for informational purpose only.

HOPE & ANECDOTES

From Page 28

- **Admit** that what was done to slaves was wrong.
- **Accept** responsibility for the actions and the resulting fallout.
- **Apologize** to the descendents of those who were killed.
- **Atone** for the sins by monetizing the slaves sacrifice.
- **Agree** to make laws to make it impossible to happen again.
- **Abolish** any laws that still exist that were illegal to begin with.
- **Arrange** for sensitivity training for everyone who benefitted.

From Page 31

- **Change** laws and policies to elevate workers above the poverty line.
- **Correct** the mindset that capitalism is better than inclusion.
- **Conform** to a wage model of that benefits workers and their families.
- **Challenge** every person in power to participate in equal pay practices.
- **Comply** with the living wage labor laws once they are enacted.
- **Compensate** workers with a livable wage so it benefits everyone.
- **Cooperate** with agendas and efforts to level the playing field.

From Page 37

- **Allocate** funding to develop support groups to deal with black PTSD.
- **Apply** faith and forgiveness philosophies to help people heal from hate.
- **Associate** hate crimes with war crimes and prosecute them as such.
- **Alter** our actions in this area by providing more support systems.
- **Adjust** our thinking about slavery by abolishing all remaining laws.
- **Adjudicate** the perpetrators of hate crimes without bias.
- **Amend** the pattern of letting secret grand juries oversee hate crimes.

From Page 41

+ **Remove** any stigma in place portrayed by the media about classes.
+ **Remind** your children often that keeping up with the Joneses is a farce.
+ **Release** information about the damage this class-based culture causes.
+ **Repair** any damage by teaching your kids to be content and modest.
+ **Recover** from a class-based system by getting rid of most items.
+ **Relocate** from class-based housing to much more modest means.
+ **Refer** to everyone you know for who they are and not what they have.

From Page 45

+ **Regulate** laws when they are enacted to benefit black voter's rights.
+ **Reform** the current rigged political systems to include the people.
+ **Remove** centuries old policies and protocols that exclude voters.
+ **Reprimand** anyone including officials still using corrupt systems.
+ **Rework** the political systems at the state and federal levels.
+ **Redevelop** best practices as a standard that ensures voter inclusion.
+ **Report** abuses that occur after new systems are in place.

From Page 49

+ **Install** citizen review boards to vet anyone who applies to be an officer.
+ **Improve** relationships with residents by including them in the process.
+ **Instill** public confidence in police officers using various measures.
+ **Incorporate** prosecution as top priority when police commit crimes.
+ **Inject** federal review boards to prosecute and process at county levels.
+ **Infuse** communities with satellite police stations that welcome citizens.
+ **Inspect** prosecuting protocols for loopholes and biases and close them.

From Page 54

- **Teach** people the truth about slavery instead of hiding it..
- **Travel** to places where cotton fields existed and plantation home are.
- **Touch** on difficult subjects to give people a glimpse of what slaves felt.
- **Talk** about solutions to modern day maltreatment and make it stop.
- **Take** preventive measures to ensure every unlawful action is exposed.
- **Train** people to understand how to be sensitive to the plight of blacks.
- **Transition** from a mindset of privilege and persecution, to acceptance.

From Page 58

- **Host** town hall meetings to discuss the fallout of slavery.
- **Help** people to get beyond their PTSD from the incidents and images.
- **Heal** through support groups and open, honest dialogue.
- **Have** discussions about how lynchings and gun violence are both murder.
- **Honor** those fallen through annual programs and dedications.
- **History** will repeat itself if we do not abolish the laws from the past.
- **Hope** that God will comfort all those are affected by this atrocity.

From Page 62

- **Dedicate** efforts to help prosecute hate crimes and supremacy crimes.
- **Destroy** barriers that keep people segregated and separated.
- **Deal** with the reality of black people's past with patience and honesty.
- **Develop** programs that provide support and sustainability.
- **Don't** ignore and push aside the needs of black people still suffering.
- **Double** and triple the amount of opportunities offered to black people.
- **Doors** are meant to be opened, open them and don't shut blacks out.

From Page 66

+ **Uproot** anything growing that is trying to rewind us to segregation.
+ **Unite** via social media & other platforms to stay connected to the cause.
+ **Unify** with other like-minded people in peaceful protest over racism.
+ **Urgency** needs to be underlined because of the political climate.
+ **Utilize** every resource available to ensure that the fight continues on.
+ **Un-educate** the mis-educated and teach them real history in America.
+ **Use** prayer, patience, and persistence because it will eventually pay off.

From Page 72

+ **Prayer** changes things when we are all on one accord and of one voice.
+ **Pause** for moments of silent prayer to remember the past and the present.
+ **Patience** has enabled us to come this far, let us not stop moving forward.
+ **Persistence** is what pushed us from the back of the bus to driving it.
+ **Passion** only works when it is directed at exactly what needs to change.
+ **Purpose** helps us understand our place in the grand scheme of things.
+ **Power** can only be received when those who have it share it or lose it.

From Page 76

+ **Forgive** those who trespass against you so that you can also be forgiven.
+ **Forge** new ground, new pathways, new businesses, new relationships.
+ **Fashion** new ideas, new products, new commodities, new networks.
+ **Forget** not where we come from but rather focus on where we are going.
+ **Force** each other to be accountable to one another inside our village.
+ **Free** our minds through learning and re-education by using the library.
+ **Fret** not thyself because of evil doers because they will soon be cut off.

From Page 80

- **Equality** emerges when all doors to wealth and wisdom are opened.
- **Equity** is the lifeblood of ownership in real estate and the road to riches.
- **Evolution** placed us 400 years behind but we had to start somewhere.
- **Energy** and exercise of our minds is how we get and remain effective.
- **Entrepreneurship** is a proven technique to use to wrangle wealth.
- **Elevation** only happens starting on the bottom & working our way up.
- **Earning** a dollar at a time is wise but it will not make you wealthy.

From Page 84

- **Organize** people who are willing to peacefully stand up for their rights.
- **Observe** the patterns & plans of racists in order to come against them.
- **Outlast** oppressive policies and laws in order to work to defeat them.
- **Outvote** bigoted agendas and campaigns in all sorts of elections.
- **Outwit** hate driven individuals and groups by thinking steps ahead.
- **Outshine** hatred with love, joy, peace, kindness and forgiveness.
- **Outperform** racists at every level so that you win each and every race.

From Page 90

- **Make** it your mission to help put an end to racism, hatred and oppression.
- **Meet** other people where they are not where you think they should be.
- **Measure** the character of person with something other than your eyes.
- **Mitigate** all issues with fairness rather than using one-sided policies.
- **Mold** and shape your children to love people no matter their color.
- **Mourn** with the families when black people are killed without cause.
- **Motivate** others with your good works so they will see it and reciprocate.

From Page 94

- **Believe** that things can be better then help work to make it happen.
- **Break** through all ignorance by hanging welcome signs in your window.
- **Branch** out and share your love with others so love grows and grows.
- **Bless** people of all races, creed, color, sexual orientation, when you can.
- **Burn** signs in your mind when you see them so they don't affect you.
- **Burst** out and laugh when you see signs of hate so it won't anger you.
- **Be** the one to always take the high road and leave hate beneath you.

From Page 98

- **Statistics** prove and history shows black people wrongfully convicted.
- **Swallow** your pride and anger in order to forgive those who abuse you.
- **Shout** to yourself the words *I'M FREE* even if you're incarcerated.
- **Strategize** on how to keep your focus away from revenge at all times.
- **Soar** above your circumstances no matter what situation you're in.
- **Stay** prayed up and peaceful, so you will be content in your circumstance.
- **Strip** away the stigma layer by layer until you are free to function again.

From Page 102

- **Resilience** is standing your ground in spite of what others do to you.
- **Rejection** is part of being black. Keep knocking until a door opens.
- **Refuse** to give up no matter how badly hateful people treat you.
- **Refer** to testimony of others who overcame what you're going through.
- **Read** the Bible for strength, stamina, endurance and longsuffering.
- **Revenge** is for people who want to become like those who oppress you.
- **Repair** damage to your reputation if you can, if not, keep moving forward.

From Page 108

- + Trust in God is the most important weapon in the war against racism.
- + Torture can't win over non-violence protests and standing up for rights.
- + Treat everyone with honor and respect even if they don't deserve it.
- + Think of others more highly than yourself & teach kids to do the same.
- + Treasure everyone you know as if they are pure gold and diamonds.
- + Take time to inform the younger generation about the past history.
- + Teach the truth no matter how damaging and hurtful it is to set us free.

From Page 112

- + Cash is king in this society and black people have been kept from it.
- + Corporate colleagues have helped one another get and stay on top.
- + Collaboration across multiple industries kept black people out.
- + Collectors have benefitted from items black people have never owned.
- + Cushioning the blow with welfare is a slap in the face to black people.
- + Catalysts like nonprofits were created to respond to greed & need.
- + Coins trickle down to black people in the form of Affirmative Action.

From Page 116

- + Inventions are supposed to benefit the inventor. Work to make it so.
- + Innovation ignites, inspires, increases, and should also include blacks.
- + Inspire all people to make like better for all not just white Americans.
- + Ignite our youth by showing them black people's contributions.
- + Improve processes and products for the masses and re-patent them.
- + Incorporate with others so you always have a team approach.
- + Include our elders in the process so they can pass on their wisdom.

From Page 120

- **Love** crushes hate, conquers color, embraces excellence, in all people.
- **Leadership** should not be a prerequisite for murderers or martyrs.
- **Life** is a gift from God and no man should have the ability to return it.
- **Leveraging** assets should include value black people bring to the table.
- **Loss** prepares for gain, but will blacks see a return for our sacrifices.
- **Litmus** is a moral test that black people aced centuries ago.
- **Losing** loved ones hurts, but blacks believe in healing and forgiveness.

From Page 126

- **Justify** all charges and convictions through an unbiased process.
- **Juries** should hear all the evidence not just what is picked by judges.
- **Justice** can only happen if the officials involved in it are unbiased.
- **Jails** are full of black people there behind excessive and false charges.
- **Judicial** process should never be in the hands of secret grand juries.
- **Join** in the fight against judicial corruption to bring justice to everyone.
- **Jesus** Christ was falsely accused, convicted, sentenced & murdered.

From Page 130

- **Government** is responsible for the plight of many people post prison.
- **Gather** all the skills you can & use your gifts & talents where you can.
- **Grace** is rarely used in post-prison decisions but it should be used often.
- **Greed** is the primary reason for wanting to keep black people in prison.
- **Groups** exist that can help ex-offenders reintegrate into society.
- **Gain** ground by knocking on every door you can until one opens.
- **Goals** are never met until and unless steps are taken to meet them.

From Page 134

- **Work** diligently to dispel myths about black people and housing..
- **Wait** patiently for perceptions to change but continuously advocate.
- **Walk** in your communities so that people will know you and yours.
- **Welcome** neighbors during annual events such as national night out.
- **Witnessing** oppression should compel you to want to help stop it.
- **Whites** are historically fearful of black people for no real reason at all.
- **Wisdom** knowledge and understanding can go a long way in this battle.

From Page 138

- **Newness** comes when old ways are no longer setting the precedent..
- **Nothing** keeps bigotry alive except whites with hatred in their hearts.
- **New** policies should always benefit today and tomorrow's Americans.
- **NAFTA** was intended to benefit all countries inside the agreement.
- **National** standards should improve the lives of citizens not burden them.
- **Never** put your life in the hands of any person who wants to end it.
- **Nobility** is earned doing good, not by being rewarded for being racist.

From Page 144

- **Keys** to happiness in a society is when all citizens are able to benefit.
- **Kites** can fly high and far away if there is no string holding them down.
- **Killers** use various methods of ending someone's life, I know that now.
- **Killing** black people for sport gave many white Americans gold medals.
- **Kindness** is the foundation of every relationship, but it is not black reality.
- **Kingdoms** can only stand when every citizen is able to participate.
- **Knowledge** of your enemy is effective when used to elevate each other.

From Page 148

- **Quit** participating in biased activities that do not include all races.
- **Quiet** voices cannot be heard; be vocal to let others know of problems.
- **Quick** methods of reaching the masses include social media groups.
- **Quiz** yourself and your family and friends to see if you have prejudice.
- **Quilts** are a fantastic way to remember contributions of black people.
- **Qualms** are expected when you are nervous, but speak out anyway.
- **Quirks** are natural feelings, being treated inhumanely is not.

From Page 152

- **Voices** raised in unison to unite against injustice is a powerful force.
- **Vocalize** through protest and demonstrations but keep it peaceful.
- **Visit** memorials and museums to show support and to remind others.
- **Value** was placed on black people to sell into slavery with no recourse.
- **Virtue** no longer exists when you treat people as if they are not people.
- **Violation** of anyone's human and civil rights makes *all* people angry.
- **Victory** is not yet won, but will be ours when glory finally does come.

From Page 156

- **Accept** that blacks started on the bottom and help them rise from there.
- **Areas** where you can assist in breaking through glass ceilings, do so.
- **Acclimate** toward industries where they are still fighting for equality.
- **Agree** that whites are responsible for and benefit from black slavery.
- **Argue** for fairness and equality in every facet of society until it happens.
- **Access** avenues where blacks are still being prevented from entering.
- **Attitude** of gratitude is the foundation and forgiveness is the force.

From Page 162

- **Banish** bias & bigotry by breaking through barriers & building balance.
- **Bury** bias and bigotry inside businesses that still hold on to such policies.
- **Bring** every race to the table in discussions that affect all Americans.
- **Build** bridges that provide pathways to promise, prosperity & provision.
- **Believe** that united we stand and divided we most certainly will fall.
- **Bravery** and boldness is what started the fight for civil & human rights.
- **Benefits** come to everyone when everyone is allowed to be beneficial.

From Page 166

- **Coalesce** with each other to help uncover patterns of patient testing.
- **Cooperate** with lawyers and advocates finding evidence of experiments.
- **Communicate** and compare stories across social media to uncover it.
- **Challenge** the government to release information on the secret labs.
- **Change** the laws so that people can be prosecuted and testing can stop.
- **Counsel** each other via support groups to help start the healing process.
- **Coordinate** national efforts to help bring this issue to the forefront.

From Page 170

- **Demonizing** black people is common in America. We see it won't end.
- **Dangerous** people with hatred in their hearts are in powerful positions.
- **Dedicating** our lives to making life better for everyone is our focus.
- **Destruction** of black slaves is not the end for their descendents.
- **Death** of black leaders is not the end for their children and grand-kids.
- **Document** each and every incident to always keep a record of history.
- **Defeat** is simply an opportunity to come back even stronger next time.

From Page 174

- **Protesting** raises our voices, rioting and looting simply silences them.
- **Peaceful** demonstrations were key to victory in the fight for civil rights.
- **People** who hate because of people who hate are like people who hate.
- **Presidents** should not be racist but rather compassionate to all citizens.
- **Protect** yourself and family from those who want you dead or enslaved.
- **Proclaim** freedom for those who never saw it in those of us left behind.
- **Partner** with peacemakers standing against what is wrong in America.

From Page 182

- **Compliance** is one way to calm a crowd, but it doesn't remove the threat.
- **Cowards** choose to hide behind their methods of madness & mayhem.
- **Cancer** comes in many forms and two of them are bigotry and bias.
- **Crowds** can gather for either good or to do evil, which one is your choice.
- **Cocktails** are meant for drinking, not used to burn down buildings.
- **Creating** fear in some can be turned into cultivating freedom for all.
- **Coercion** was just one of the tactics used in slavery still used today.

From Page 186

- **Fire** can burn forever, just like the bigotry and bias lit long ago.
- **Freedom** stands firmly in the face of and fights against fascism.
- **Fresh** ideas come from forward think not backwards attitudes & antics.
- **From** the beginning of the colonization of the U.S. hatred has harmed.
- **Fallacies** cloud a sane person's ideals and turns them into illusions.
- **Flames** create light to illuminate the darkness around it, ironic isn't it?
- **Fractions** are simply part of the whole of a collective in a common factor.

From Page 190

+ **Hours** mark the turn of the clock, and many wish to turn it backwards.
+ **Hurt** never heals as long as the scab covering it keeps being picked at.
+ **How** can we all move forward when one group won't move out the way.
+ **Hasten** to the triage that is a hospital and help for the spiritually sick.
+ **Horrific** images of hatred past and present hurt me, do they upset you?
+ **Honesty** is always the best policy even when its built on layers of lies.
+ **Hear** the men, women & children who sacrificed their lives for all of us.

From Page 194

+ **Malice** lives in the hearts of those who hate and hurt others for no reason.
+ **Murder** is their method and madness and mayhem is their motivation.
+ **Moving** north no longer makes us safe because it has spread everywhere.
+ **Maligned** from north to south, east to west, no place is immune from it.
+ **Meaningless** murders take place everywhere, even in our children still.
+ **Mourning** & grieving will never satisfy the never-ending pain we feel.
+ **Mending** the scars with strength is still our band-aid after the burial.

From Page 202

+ **Ignoring** evidence & moving forward in spite of is difficult but necessary.
+ **Initiate** new paths to progress, race forward and don't run backwards.
+ **Instill** faith, hope and charity in your children and teach them to pray.
+ **Inject** truth into all you do, and let lies & legends fall where they may.
+ **Increase** and enlarge your territory through Biblical and social circles.
+ **Insist** upon doing the right thing and don't settle for anything less.
+ **Inhale** the power, take in the promise, and learn to exhale the problems.

From Page 206

- **Torches** are meant to burn, but we can use them to light our way.
- **Testimony** can help others get through, what you have gone through.
- **Talk** to each other so that you can listen and learn from one another.
- **Task** yourself each day to push higher, work harder, and pray stronger.
- **Time** heals all wounds, but only if you bring the hurt to the surface.
- **Turning** the other cheek shows they didn't hurt you with the first blow.
- **Terminate** any thoughts to retaliate but rather restore what they destroy.

From Page 210

- **Sunshine** even on an overcast day, still provides light for you to look at.
- **Staying** relaxed, resilient, resolute, reticent, helps you reverence God.
- **Soothing** yourself by going camping is how I kept my family focused.
- **Strength** can come from recharging your battery by getting outdoors.
- **Spending** time outside eases your mind and helps you focus inside.
- **Senses** respond to what you show them, may it always be peaceful.
- **Specialize** in keeping soft sounds and music, around you at all times.

From Page 214

- **Effective** & effectual are two words taught about prayer in James 5:16.
- **Energizing** through rest and relaxation keeps you peaceful & powerful.
- **Educate** others on how to stop focusing and fretting over evil people.
- **Emerge** victorious and you will spend little time worried about others.
- **Eat** from scripture and it will strengthen your spirit inside and out.
- **East** is just one point on a compass, there are three more to explore.
- **Everything** around you is not meant for you to see or hear. Turn it off.

There is a growing number of
people of color
in America.

There is a growing number of
wealthy black Americans.

There is a growing number of
diverse churches
in America.

There is a growing number of
people of color in politics
in America.

There is a growing number of
diverse schools
in America.

I say all this to say
we simply need to keep moving forward
one day at a time
knowing that we are still in the struggle
for equality and human and civil rights
and because of how America started
there will never truly be an end.

CLOSING THOUGHTS

I'm not by any stretch of the imagination a new author. I've been writing my entire life. I've been publishing professionally since my feature articles began appearing on the front pages of my local black newspaper in 1993, and I was paid for my literature and labor.

Most of my works have been geared toward helping people to better navigate the Christian lifestyle, business, ethics, education and technology.

I felt compelled to author this work because I grew tired of holding it all in. I've held this text within me, incubating for decades due to my refusal to feed into the rhetoric without any real results.

Then my direction and focus changed, which showed me a different audience, and it placed me in the front of the right eyes instead of the intended black and white ones.

When you systematically suppress the value and contribution of other groups of people simply because the color of their skin is different, there is something seriously sinister about you and you are not to be trusted.

I continue to pray that God will intervene and send His army to come and destroy sin and selfishness once and for all, *and that He would do it very soon.*

Be Blessed.
Keith M. Hammond

BLACK BOY
"Dad, why do white people hate us so much?"

BLACK MAN
"It's not us son, they hate who and what they see in us."

BLACK BOY
"Is that the reason many of them try to be like us?"

BLACK MAN
"Imitation is the sincerest form of flattery son."

BLACK BOY
"Is that why they tan to get our skin color?
Why so many speak and try to talk like us.
And why they make music to try and sing and sound like us?
And what about when they wear clothes to try and dress like us?
They even change their hair to look like ours...seems clear to me!"

BLACK MAN
**"Many of them want what we have but they don't want *us* to have it.
Their history is to kill what they cannot conquer or control.
Or they commercialize it and find a way to profit from it."**

BLACK BOY
"But they *have* everything. They stole this land. They steal lots of money.
And they literally own just about everything. They even owned *US* before.
Why aren't they ever satisfied?"

BLACK MAN
**"Greed has no boundary or ending. Steal, kill and destroy has been
their way of life for so long that they don't know anything else."**

BLACK BOY
"So all the stealing and killing, lying and covering it up will never end?"

BLACK MAN
**"We don't believe it will, but we remain hopeful son.
Hatred lives in their heart, and it is deeply rooted.
Many of them have changed. But for others it seems to be easier
to kill what reminds them of their history, and that my son, is *us*."**

BLACK BOY
"Dad, thanks for explaining all this to me.
I've learned a very valuable lesson."

BLACK MAN
"What is that my son?"

BLACK BOY
"They seem to want what we have,
but I would never want what they have."

BLACK MAN
"Correct my son. Because their history, without help from Heaven,
will lead them straight to Hell."

www.ingramcontent.com/pod-product-compliance
Lightning Source LLC
Chambersburg PA
CBHW071154160426
43196CB00011B/2077